Mag•ic (măj′ik) *noun.* **1**. the ability to make ordinary moments astonishing, awe-inspiring, exciting, and fun **2**. a demonstration that is spectacular, emotionally moving, and unforgettable **3**. a feeling of amazement and wonder

Illustrations By: Accentia Technologies

Special thanks to Rebekah South, Jessica South, Christie Block, Spencer South, Kylie Ahlschwede, Melinda Turner, Desiree Farley, Veronica Kaletta, Melanie Holdaway, Janele Williams, Rachel Curley, Emma Andersen, Noah Andersen, Rebecca Turner

Dedicated to all the teachers that go the extra mile
to inspire their students and will never completely
know how much they have touched their lives.

Thank you, Mrs. Morgan*

*In case you were wondering, Mrs. Morgan was my 4th grade teacher. She made sure I never
felt like less of a person because of my weaknesses (mostly spelling and reading) and encouraged
me to follow my dream of being a professional magician. She allowed me to do book reports on
magic and perform little magic shows for the entire class. She even drove 40 miles to try to get
me tickets to a sold out David Copperfield show. She was amazing, and I can honestly say you
might not be holding this book right now if it weren't for her understanding and encouragement.
- Brian Daniel, founder of TeachByMagic.com

Pick a card, any card.

Memorize the shape and color on your card
and then turn the page.

I will now turn all the cards over,
mix them up, and set one aside.

Would you be impressed if
I removed the same card you chose?
Turn to the next page to see
if I got it right.

Is your card missing?

Awesome, I thought so....
Turn the page one last time, and I'll
show you how I knew all along
which card you would choose.

5

WELCOME TO TEACH BY MAGIC!

Our goal with Teach by Magic is to provide you with a storehouse of useful, incredibly easy-to-do magic tricks using inexpensive props. Most of the tricks can be done with materials you already have available or which can be purchased at your local supermarket for only a dollar or two. Most importantly, we have created the website www.TeachByMagic.com as an online resource to help you find the perfect trick for any situation as quickly and easily as possible.

Learning starts with wonder!

Wonder is the greatest key to learning. The human race, by nature, wonders about everything! We wonder why there are stars in the sky or how acorns grow into trees. We read books and watch movies because we wonder if good will overcome evil. We watch sports because we wonder which team will win. We feel wonder whenever we experience new and amazing things, and that wonder leads to curiosity. Curiosity, in turn, is what drives us to seek answers to the things we wonder about, which is how we learn! We want the children in your classroom to experience wonder because it makes them care about the subject you're teaching. And that makes them want to learn.

Wondering about that card trick?

We could have started this book in numerous ways; a table of contents maybe, or the story of how Teach By Magic got started. You might have even been expecting a few pages of facts and scientific research that show how teaching with magic can improve students' retention of information by involving more of their five senses in the learning process. We could easily fill countless pages with that kind of information. But let's be honest—is that what you want to read? Of course not! Odds are that you already know all that, and, seriously, do we have to do research to know that we learn more when we're having fun? We wanted to start this book with an experience that would make you wonder. Don't worry—we'll explain how that card trick worked next.

The magic behind the magic.

The Secret! That's the element most responsible for making magic so cool! So how did we know which card you would select from so many possible choices? We didn't. We still don't. That would be impossible! The secret is: we cheated. We knew that if we asked you to select just one card from a lot of different options, you would memorize one card without paying much attention to all the other ones. So on the subsequent page we changed all the cards to different ones that didn't exist before. Every single one.

 Although they're similar in appearance, none of the cards on page five are exactly the same as the cards on page one. So no matter which card you choose, you won't find it again later. Sneaky, isn't it?

That seems too simple!

The magic tricks in this book and on the website are all easy to do. That's good from a performing standpoint, but it can dampen your enthusiasm in a way. When we see something that instills wonder in us, we expect there to be a complicated explanation requiring highly-technical skills, years of practice, and a behind-the-curtain arrangement of smoke and mirrors to pull it off. Contrary to popular belief, most magicians only use mirrors in their dressing rooms to check their hair. To fully appreciate the wonder created by any given trick, it's always best to watch and experience it from the audience's point of view before you learn the secret. Then you know that the trick works, so when you think, "This is just too simple," you can remember how much it amazed you the first time you saw it. Therefore, we strongly recommend that you go to www.TeachByMagic.com/BOOK and watch the presentation for each trick before learning how it works. We know from our own experience that once you know how a trick is done, it will never have the same impact as it does when you see it performed for the first time.

Why keep the secret?

The secret to a magic trick is even more important than the "whodunnit" in a mystery novel. The magic secrets you are learning in this book should be respected and kept. The truth is that learning secrets to magic can be disappointing. People think they want to know the secret, but ignorance really is bliss. We liken it to Santa Claus. Santa is magical and filled with wonder and excitement, not only for children but for their parents as well. When a child stops believing in Santa, that magic and wonder go away, and it is much less fun for everyone.

How do I keep the secret?

The best defense is a good offense. It's important to be prepared for the occasional interrogation, but it's best to avoid it if you can, so try to present the tricks in such a way that the mystery is exciting rather than frustrating. And it's always a good idea to be ready to go right into something else. But if a student does come up to you with the classic question, "How did you do that?" here are a few fun responses:

- "I made a promise not to tell anyone.
  You wouldn't want me to break my promise, would you?"
- "I can't show you how I did that one, but if you finish your
  work I can show you a different one."
- "I was hoping you knew so you could tell me."
- "I'll tell you when you are 21."
- "Lucky for you, you don't need to know how that was done
  to pass the class, but you do need to know...."
- "I ate all my vegetables as a child."
- "The question is not how I did it, but why..." and go right into the real reason.
- "Can you keep a secret? So can I!"

Wait, aren't you breaking your own rule?

Yes, we're revealing secrets. But, no, we're not breaking our rule. Think of it as giving out information on a "need to know" basis. If someone wants to know how a trick is done just out of curiosity, that's a compliment that the performer did a good job. But going around telling everyone who asks is just exposure, and it ruins the fun for everyone. On the other hand, if someone wants to know the secret so they can perform the trick themselves, that's a different situation. In this case, for example, you want to learn some tricks to use in your classroom to bring joy to others and help them learn, so sharing some secrets is totally fine.

Are there some tricks I can teach my students?

Great question! Yes, there are. Learning magic is fun and can build self-esteem; it may even become a healthy hobby for some of your students. We have quite a few tricks and puzzles that will benefit your students even more if they learn how to do them. Tricks like Calculator Cards (pg. 48) and Wonder Bottle (pg. 74) will involve your students more, and they're great tricks to take home and perform for others. They'll be happy to do that homework! Make sure they understand the importance of keeping the secret to themselves, though. Your students may have little brothers or sisters who will also be in your classroom one day. You want the experience to be new and fresh for them as well!

Some tricks like the Magnetic Hand (pg. 18) or Remote Control Paper (pg. 38) could be used as an incentive. Show them the trick and then teach them the secret as a reward for getting their homework done on time or for good behavior. And, of course, many of the tricks are challenges where the solution or secret is given as part of the presentation. For example, Rectangle Squared (pg. 47), Water Tower (pg. 70), and all the tricks in the Challenge section (pgs. 26-31).

But you should never use tricks like Magic Mailer (pg. 20), Cut and Restored Balloon (pg. 22), or Never Wrong, Always Write (pg. 56) as an incentive or reward. There is no reason to share the secret. If you tell your students how these tricks are done, no positive results can come from it. All you will accomplish is to eliminate the wonder that makes them work as a tool for learning.

What if I have some students or parents who avoid "magic" for religious or personal reasons?

It's important to point out that the magic in this book is very different from the "magic" that many religions teach their members to avoid, which is also called witchcraft, sorcery, or wizardry. A good comparison is the use of the word "drugs." For good reason, we are taught at an early age to "say 'no' to drugs." Drugs are bad for you. However, if a child has a headache and you want her to take some children's aspirin, you would never say, "Do you want some drugs?" even though aspirin is a useful, helpful drug.

The magic in this book consists exclusively of tricks, puzzles, and illusions. The tricks may amaze, entertain, or motivate the students, but they're all based on rational scientific principles. They have absolutely no connection to anything supernatural or evil, and they should never be presented that way. Magic for entertainment is a respected art form akin to dance, theater, music, puppetry, or juggling. However, a child who is taught that "magic" is bad may find it difficult to know the difference. Just as you wouldn't offer "drugs" to a child, it's a good idea to choose your words carefully if you feel one of your students might misunderstand the material you are presenting.

How will I know if I have a student that falls into this category?
As a general rule of thumb, if you have a child that does not celebrate Halloween or is not allowed to read books about famous wizarding schools, you probably should avoid using any form of the word "magic."

What term should I use instead of "magic?"
What you're learning in this book can be called many things: tricks, puzzles, stunts, demonstrations, object lessons, brain teasers, challenges, or—our favorite—illusions. We like "illusion" because that is exactly what we are creating: a perception of something that only exists in the mind. We are tricking the brain, but there is always a scientific and logical explanation for what is being seen. If you use the word "illusion," you might want to demonstrate several optical illusions so that the class members learn to associate illusion with the concept of tricking the brain. You can even teach your class the meaning of illusion when you introduce your first lesson.

How do I actually incorporate these tricks into my lessons?

As an attention getter

Many of the tricks in Teach By Magic are designed to grab attention and get everyone on the same page. A quick magic trick to introduce a lesson is a great way to make sure your students are ready to watch, listen, and learn. We have found this to be useful for both the start of a new topic and for emphasizing points throughout the topic. If your students know that you might use a magic trick at any time, they are likely to pay closer attention to every lesson because they don't want to miss a magic moment.

As an incentive or reward

Tricks from Teach By Magic can be used as incentives in a couple of ways. When dealing with tricks whose secrets should be guarded, you can say, "I will show you a fun trick once everyone is finished," or, "If we make it through the whole day with no names on the board, I will show you something amazing." When using tricks and challenges that you can teach your students, you can demonstrate the trick at the start of the lesson with the promise that if the students complete their assignments (or meet whatever goal you set for them), you will teach them how to do the trick at the end of the lesson.

As an easy and fun way to review

Magic makes reviewing a fun process, rather than a burdensome chore. It helps both the students who already have a firm grasp of the information and those who have either forgotten or never quite got it in the first place. Students who have retained the information tend to tune out. A magic trick will spice up the review and keep their attention. Those who still need to learn the material will have the chance to learn it in a different and more memorable way.

As an integrated part of the lesson

Probably the most common way to use Teach By Magic is as an object lesson so that the trick actually illustrates and emphasizes one or more of the main ideas. For example, if you are teaching about the freezing point of water, you can magically make ice appear when water is poured into a cup with the words "32 degrees Fahrenheit" written on it. This helps your students learn and remember that water freezes at 32 degrees Fahrenheit. Bet you want to know how that is done, don't you? See? Teach By Magic works! See page 68 for the explanation.

As a way to build relationships with your students

Our experience is that teachers will find many ways to use Teach by Magic. We conclude this short discussion with our favorite: magic is a great way to connect and bond with others. It transcends language barriers and cultural differences, and can even put a smile on the shiest of children. The important thing is that you are the one doing the trick. It's important that they connect the cool moment to you and not to a video. **Avoid the temptation to just show the videos from TeachByMagic.com.** Children can watch videos at home. We want the students to bond with you; we want you to be the star.

I've never performed magic before. I'm nervous!

Many people are uncomfortable performing in public, especially with something they've never done before. It doesn't help that magic tricks often seem like they have to be performed perfectly or else they'll be a complete failure. The good news is that, most of the time, the props do all the hard work for you. In addition, the audience has no idea what the trick is supposed to look like. They only know how you act (or react!) when you do the trick. And performing magic isn't brain surgery or rocket science—there won't be any casualties if a trick doesn't end precisely as you intended.

You'll find that after two or three tricks, your confidence will build, and you'll want to do more. Every contributor to this book and every performer on the website went through exactly the same thing! Meanwhile, here are a few tips to get you off to a smooth start.

Pick easier tricks to start – There's no reason to make yourself do a back flip if you can do jumping jacks instead. At www.TeachByMagic.com you can search and sort the tricks by difficulty so you can make sure you're starting with easier ones. Some of the easier tricks to perform in this book are:

- Linking Paperclips (pg. 90)
- Rectangle Squared (pg. 47)
- Airmail (pg. 31)
- Adding Time (pg. 46)

Practice, practice, practice! – The more times you run through it, the more comfortable you'll feel and the less likely you'll be to do something wrong. Try running through the demonstration exactly the way you would do it in your classroom, word for word. You may want to practice in front of a mirror so you can see how things look from the students' point of view.

Show a friendly spectator first – Showing the trick to a spouse, to one of your own children, or to a friend will help. Having performed it once for a real person always makes you feel more confident.

Plan for mistakes – Just like anything else in life, sooner or later there will be mistakes. Even the greatest magicians in Las Vegas have an occasional failure. Our best advice is to plan ahead because it will happen to you, too. But if you're prepared you'll be a lot less concerned about it. Here are a few ways to handle such situations:

- Start over - If the mistake is reversible or if the trick hasn't gone beyond the "point-of-no-return," you can simply begin again. Clap your hands together Hollywood-style, say, "Take Two!" and give it another go.

- End it like you meant it - If the trick has gotten its message across or is at least a partial victory, go with it. Nobody knows what was supposed to happen except you! Summarize the important concepts taught and ignore the petty details.

- Magic takes time - If something isn't working and you can afford to wait, tell the class that magic takes time sometimes and you'll check again later. Maybe two parts of a trick are supposed to come together but aren't cooperating (like the Wonder Bottle, pg. 74). Give it a few minutes and try again or wait until recess to correct the problem and finish the trick after the class comes back. Or perhaps there are too many slices (or too few!) in your sliced banana (Karate Banana, pg. 44). If too many, say, "I should have peeled that a little quicker!" For too few, say, "I should have let that sit just a moment longer."

- Laugh, live, and learn - If the trick is a complete and obvious failure, laugh! You can be sure the class will still learn what you're trying to teach because you will have their undivided attention! Then turn it into a lesson of a different sort. Tell them, "You know, there's something else to be learned. Life isn't perfect, and neither am I!" How you react to the situation will actually help the students feel better when they have problems of their own, and they'll respect you for accepting the way things turned out.

Never repeat a trick - Magicians strictly adhere to this rule. This is because the second time you perform a trick, your students know what to expect and are more likely to catch the secret. It's always a good idea to spread out similar tricks. For example, we wouldn't recommend using a Wonder Bag (pg. 66) every other day—your students might catch on that something is funny about that bag, and they'll have more chances to sneak a peek at it. But if you wait a month or two, you can pull it back out and do something different with it. NOTE: There are some tricks that have you repeating them for the presentation, like Word Warp (pg. 40) and Balancing Card (pg. 84). This is fine because it's part of the design to do it over and over again.

Act naturally – Again, the best defense is a good offense. If your students don't suspect there is a secret, they won't be thinking they know how it's done. The most common hurdle for those new to magic is acting like nothing funny is going on when something funny is. For example, with the Appearing Ruler (pg. 19), you have a ruler hidden up your sleeve or behind your watch. It's really easy to act funny because you know you're hiding something. If you show the class an item that's used every day —box, bag, bowl, cup, paper—they'll assume it's as normal as any other. If you say, "I am going to pour water into this ordinary cup," (Instant Ice, pg. 68) the word "ordinary" might make your students think, "Hey, maybe it's not." It's very important to remember that if you don't tell your class, "Now I am going to do a trick," they have no reason to suspect you are going to trick them. They have no idea what to expect or what to look for. The last thing they are going to think is that you have a measuring device up your sleeve.

What if one of my students knows the secret to the trick?

This may happen, but it's more likely that your student only thinks he knows the secret. One of our presenters had a child come up to him after a show, once and, with dozens of others watching, this little guy says, "Mr. Magician, I know how you made that ball float."   It could have been an embarrassing situation, but he looked at the boy and said, "Really? So how did I do it?" all the while sweating over what he might suggest—strings, magnets, mirrors, a flying monkey...who knows! And then the boy said, "You used your magical powers, and you held your hands like this!"

The moral of the story is that kids will be kids; you never know what they will say. The thing to do here is not let it get to you. Just plan on it happening occasionally and be prepared with what you are going to say. For example, "That's good, because I don't know how it's done. Maybe later you can come whisper it in my ear." Or, "WOW, you do? That's really great. Can you keep a secret?...That's good, because we don't want to ruin the fun for others."

One last, IMPORTANT, tip.

Have you heard the expression, "Possession is nine-tenths of the law?" Well, PRESENTATION is nine-tenths of the magic. If you were to read a book with no enthusiasm, no intonations, and without different voices for the different characters, it wouldn't be very engaging. In the interest of space, the presentations we give you for all the tricks in the book are very simple; they're just the raw elements. Don't be afraid to really dress up the tricks and have fun with them. The more you embellish the trick, the more effective it will be and the more disguised the secret will be.

The way you say and present things can completely change the way the trick is perceived. For example, let's go back to that flash card trick in the beginning of the book.   "Turn the page one last time, and I'll show you how I knew all along which card you would choose."   By saying, "I knew all along," it implies that we knew which card you would select even before you selected it. This makes the trick more believable because, hey, maybe there's some psychology involved that makes everyone pick the same card. So there's an element of believability, but it's still amazing. We can't stress this enough. The secret is just one little part of what makes magic tricks magical. The real magic is in the presentation; it's in you. Notes on paper don't make music; it's the way the musician plays those notes that makes us enjoy them.

"Grandpa took a thread and gently tied it around my finger. 'Let this string be a reminder for you to get me a ripe bunch of bananas when Grandma takes you to the market tomorrow.' I heard him, but when tomorrow came the string was gone along with any memory of our talk.

Grandpa was a little disappointed that his string trick didn't secure my memory. The next week, before the market run, Grandpa handed me a banana and said, 'Do you know why I like bananas so much?' I said, 'No, sir.' He said, 'Because every so often one of the bananas is very special. They are so special that I like to eat one each day, hoping to see the magic inside.' I said, 'What magic?' He said, 'The mystery of the sliced bananas.' My eyes could not have been wider as I wondered what mystery a banana could hold.

He said, 'I'm feeling really special today, and this might be a magical banana. I'll let you peel the banana, and if it's sliced in half, we will have good luck all day. If it's sliced into three pieces, we will have good luck all week. But if it's sliced in four pieces, then we will have good luck all year.' As I peeled the banana, I saw one slice, then two, then three. The banana was cut into four pieces. It was the best year Grandpa and I ever had. As we ate the banana, he said, 'Would you remind Grandma to get me some bananas?'"

Magic makes memories, memories inspire learning, and learning starts with wonder.

Welcome to a world of wonder for you and your students. Put yourself in the place of the child in that story. Grandpa understood how to help that child remember something important.

What if Grandpa's teaching tool is so simple that you could use it in your classroom and you could do it in less than a minute?

If you could find the solution on the next page, would you turn the page?

Well, what are you waiting for? Turn the page!

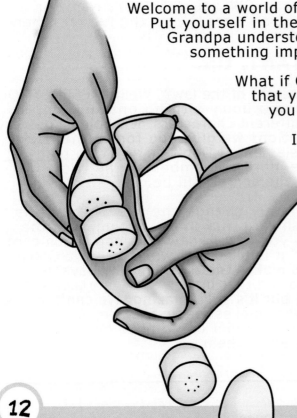

TABLE OF CONTENTS

Did You Know?

If your head were the same size as any of the heads on Mt. Rushmore, you would be nearly 500 feet tall.

ATTENTION GETTERS

Instant Knot

Illustrate that difficulties can be overcome by making a knot appear on a piece of rope.

Magnetic Hand

Grab students' attention as you introduce a lesson by making a pencil stick to your hand without any visible support!

Appearing Ruler

Introduce a lesson on measurements by pulling a large wooden ruler out of a folded envelope!

Magic Mailer

Make a paper that reads, "Today's Lesson," turn into an item from the lesson.

Cut and Restored Balloon

Cut a large hole in a balloon and then immediately inflate the balloon as if the cut had never been made. This can introduce a wide variety of subjects.

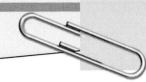

INSTANT KNOT

Objective:
Illustrate that difficulties can be overcome and that we should always "tie, tie again."

What's Seen:
A knot suddenly appears on a piece of rope. If you wish, you can make it disappear too!

Materials Needed:
• A piece of soft cotton rope about 30" long. Other types of rope can be used, but stiffer ropes don't work as well.

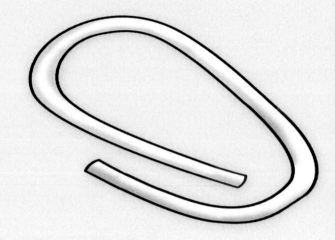

The Secret:
The knot is really there the whole time—it's just hidden in your hand. You make it "appear" when you want by simply dropping the end with the knot. You can make it "disappear" by reversing the procedure.

Preparation:
1. Secure the ends of the rope with tape or glue to prevent them from unraveling.

2. Tie a single overhand knot about six inches from one end of the rope.

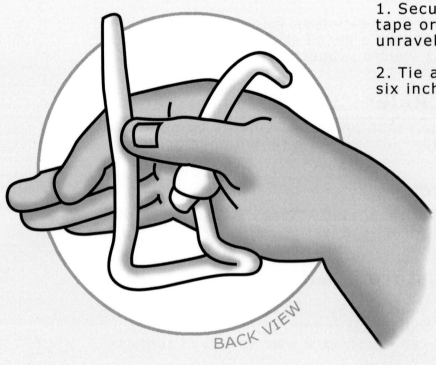

BACK VIEW

HINT:

A lot of times it's easier to learn a magic trick from watching a video because you can see exactly what it should look like. You can watch every trick in this book at www.TeachByMagic.com.

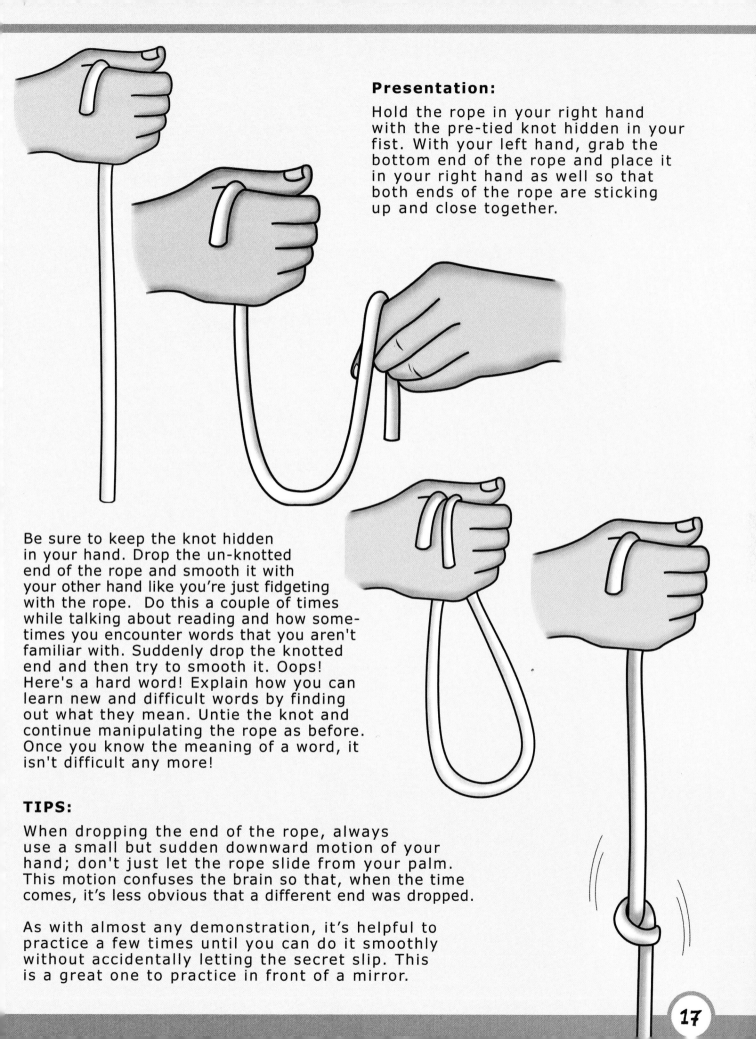

Presentation:

Hold the rope in your right hand with the pre-tied knot hidden in your fist. With your left hand, grab the bottom end of the rope and place it in your right hand as well so that both ends of the rope are sticking up and close together.

Be sure to keep the knot hidden in your hand. Drop the un-knotted end of the rope and smooth it with your other hand like you're just fidgeting with the rope. Do this a couple of times while talking about reading and how sometimes you encounter words that you aren't familiar with. Suddenly drop the knotted end and then try to smooth it. Oops! Here's a hard word! Explain how you can learn new and difficult words by finding out what they mean. Untie the knot and continue manipulating the rope as before. Once you know the meaning of a word, it isn't difficult any more!

TIPS:

When dropping the end of the rope, always use a small but sudden downward motion of your hand; don't just let the rope slide from your palm. This motion confuses the brain so that, when the time comes, it's less obvious that a different end was dropped.

As with almost any demonstration, it's helpful to practice a few times until you can do it smoothly without accidentally letting the secret slip. This is a great one to practice in front of a mirror.

MAGNETIC HAND

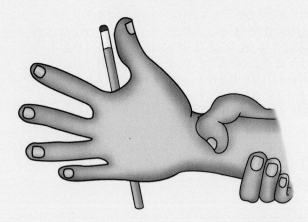

Objective:
Grab your students' attention as you introduce a lesson on magnetism, gravity, China, measuring, reading, etc.

What's Seen:
A pencil, ruler, bookmark, or other object sticks to your hand without any visible support almost as if it's floating!

Materials Needed:
• A pencil (or other applicable item)

The Secret:

The "floating" object is actually held in place with the index finger of your opposite hand while it is squeezing your wrist. Amazingly enough, most people won't notice that a finger is missing from view.

Presentation:

Depending on the lesson, your dialogue will change. Visit www.TeachByMagic.com to see different presentations of the Magnetic Hand. For example, you might make chopsticks float to introduce the subject of China or make a bookmark float to introduce a new book. As a general attention getter, you can just show off your magnetic personality.

Announce that you have a magnetic personality and that you will prove it. Show a pencil and say that you can make it stick to your hand simply by squeezing your wrist.

Rub your hand on your stomach to "magnetize" it. Then place the pencil into your fist and grab your wrist as if to steady the magnetic power that is radiating.

Say, "See? My hand is now magnetic!" and, as you move your hand around (making sure your palm is pointing away from your students), secretly move your index finger into place to secure the pencil.

Open your fist and shake your hand to show that the pencil will not fall off!

Make sure to keep the palm of your magnetic hand facing away from your students and to hold the floating object by the tip of your index finger so the object is as far away as possible from your other fingers.

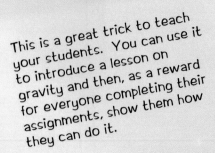

This is a great trick to teach your students. You can use it to introduce a lesson on gravity and then, as a reward for everyone completing their assignments, show them how they can do it.

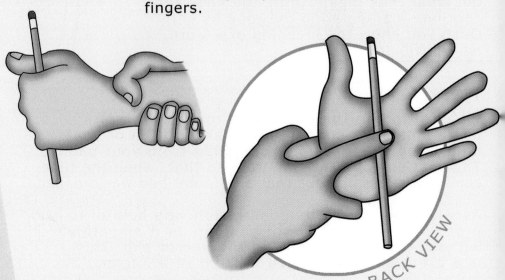

BACK VIEW

APPEARING RULER

 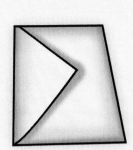 

Objective:
Introduce a lesson on measurements.

What's Seen:
A wooden ruler is pulled out of a folded envelope!

Materials Needed:
- A wooden ruler
- A business-size envelope
- A wrist watch or bracelet

The Secret:

The ruler is up your sleeve or behind your arm being held by your wrist watch! Folding the envelope beforehand makes it even more impossible for the ruler to be hidden inside it.

Preparation:

1. Fold the envelope into thirds and put it in your pocket.

2. Slide the ruler under your bracelet or watch band along your forearm. Keep one end in your palm.

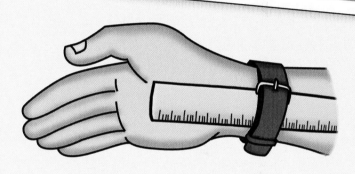

Presentation:

Pull the folded envelope out of your pocket and announce that it contains a very useful tool for measuring. Unfold it and place it in your palm so that the bottom edge is under the end of the ruler and the envelope will open towards you. Finally, open the envelope and slowly pull the ruler out! Be sure to keep the back of your hand facing the audience at all times so they can't see the ruler hidden along your forearm.

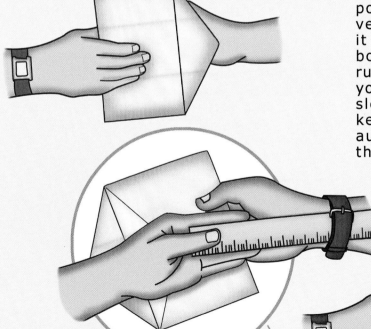

BACK VIEW

MAGIC MAILER

Objective:
Introduce the subject of today's lesson in a way that is sure to get everyone's attention.

What's Seen:
A paper that reads, "Today's Lesson," turns into an item from the lesson.

Materials Needed:
- 2 large U.S. Express or Priority Mail envelopes
- Scissors
- Glue
- Blank sheet of paper and marker
- Lesson item

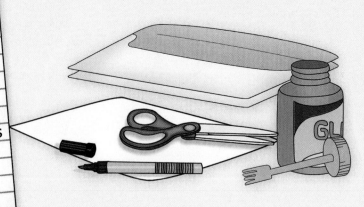

The Secret:

The "Magic Mailer" is a specially-prepared envelope that has two compartments. It can be shown empty even with a piece of paper in it, allowing you to switch any flat object for another.

Preparation:

1. Take one envelope and trim off the fold all the way down on both sides.

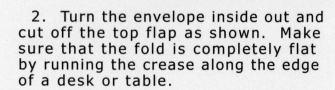

2. Turn the envelope inside out and cut off the top flap as shown. Make sure that the fold is completely flat by running the crease along the edge of a desk or table.

3. Glue the two sides together with the printed sides facing each other, creating the secret panel.

4. You may need to trim the sides and top a little more so it will fit nicely inside another envelope.

NOTE: The top of the secret flap should be about 1/8" shorter than the lower edge of the other envelope.

5. Place the panel inside the other envelope with the fold up, creating your Magic Mailer.

6. Place the lesson item you are going to make appear in place of the "Today's Lesson" paper between the loose panel and the short side of the envelope.

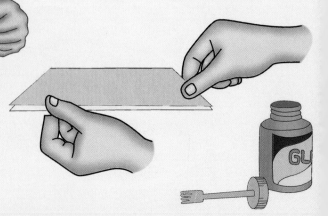

Presentation:

Announce that you don't know what the class will be learning next but you are really excited to find out. Explain that the topic for today's lesson is going to come in the mail. Show the class both sides of a blank sheet of paper and then use a marker to write, "Today's Lesson," on the paper.

Fold the paper in half and explain that you're going to put it in the magic mailer and it will come back with the lesson topic inside.

Show that the mailer is empty (hold the secret panel against the short side of the envelope, hiding the sheet that is already there), then put the "Today's Lesson" sheet inside (between the secret panel and the long side of the envelope).

Fold over the flap of the envelope to close it, but don't seal it.

Shake the envelope (to simulate travel) then announce that it has returned with the new lesson topic. Open the envelope, pull out the previously concealed lesson item with a flourish, and begin the lesson.

CUT AND RESTORED BALLOON

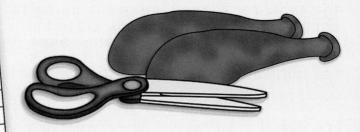

Objective:
Introduce a lesson with an unforgettable demonstration that ties directly into the subject.

What's Seen:
A large cut is made in a balloon and then the balloon is immediately inflated as if the cut had never been made.

Materials Needed:
- Two identical balloons (11" or larger)
- Scissors

The Secret:
There are actually two balloons. The second balloon is folded and hidden inside a specially-prepared balloon. When you cut the balloon, you only cut the outer one. When you blow up the inner balloon, the outer, cut balloon will gather around the neck of the inflated balloon.

Preparation:

1. Cut off the top ring from the mouth of one balloon.

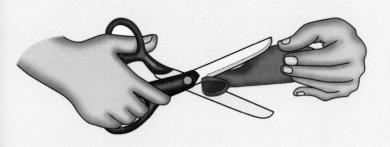

2. Take the other balloon and stretch it as if you were about to inflate it (this is the balloon you will be blowing up).

3. Now fold it onto itself, accordion style, so that most of the body of the balloon is tucked just below the neck.

NOTE: You want to make sure that the balloon isn't folded up so tightly that it's difficult to inflate, but you want it to be tucked in enough that it doesn't accidently get cut when you're doing the demonstration. Practice preparing and cutting balloons a few times until you get a good feel for it.

4. Stretch open the neck of the balloon that is missing its top rim and tuck the folded one inside of it.

5. Align the two balloons so that the cut edge of the outer balloon is against the ring of the folded one; it should now look like a single balloon.

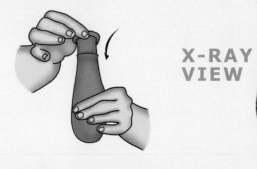

X-RAY VIEW

A Few Different Applications

English - Homophones
Explain that "hole" and "whole" sound the same but mean completely different things. Cut a "hole" in the balloon and then magically make it "whole" again.

Math - Rounding
Show the balloon and say it represents a whole number, like the number three. Cut off just a little, making it 2.7, and then "round" the balloon back up to the whole number three again.

Social Studies – Historical Heroes
Illustrate the importance of celebrating the birthdays of important people, like Martin Luther King, Jr. If we don't celebrate and remember each year, we might forget their contributions (watch this video online—it makes sense, we promise!).

Science - Asexual Reproduction
Demonstrate asexual reproduction by splitting the balloon, representing a cell, in two with the scissors and then showing how one half can grow into another totally complete cell.

Health – No Smoking
Talk about taking care of your body and how smoking damages your lungs. Show a pink balloon representing a lung and cut it to represent the damage cigarettes do. But if we don't smoke and we keep our lungs healthy, we can use them to inflate balloons, just like this one!

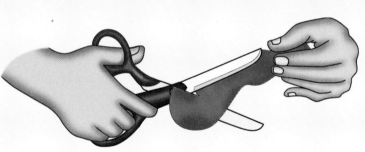

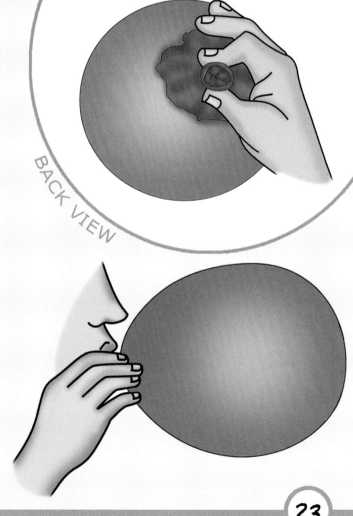

BACK VIEW

Presentation:

Introduce the day's lesson topic. A lesson on reptiles, for example, might go like this: Explain that some lizards can shed their tails when attacked by predators and then grow a new tail! As you talk about shedding the tail, cut off the bulb end of the balloon (about an inch up works fine). Make sure to show the detached piece of the balloon; you really did cut it!

Next, after talking about re-growth, blow the balloon up. The cut balloon will automatically gather around the neck of the inflated balloon, and you can simply keep it hidden in your hand. Or you can secretly remove it as you tie the balloon in a knot if you wish.

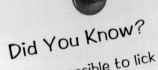

Did You Know?

It is impossible to lick your elbow.

No piece of normal-size paper can be folded in half more than 7 times.

CHALLENGES

Instant Star

Can you make a five pointed star out of broken toothpicks without touching them?

4+4=6 Puzzle

Can you arrange six coins into two rows of four?

Kirigami Ring

Can you cut a hole in a 3" x 5" index card large enough to step through?

Paper Bridge

Can you build a bridge out of a piece of paper that's strong enough to hold a ceramic mug?

Air Mail

Can you fold a postcard so that it can't be blown off a table?

INSTANT STAR

Objective:
Demonstrate capillary action or introduce an astronomy lesson.

What's Seen:
A star is made out of bent toothpicks without touching them!

Materials Needed:
- Five toothpicks
- Eyedropper or drinking straw
- Water

The Secret:
Broken and bent wooden toothpicks absorb the water by capillary action and start to straighten out. When they've straightened out enough, the ends touch and form a five-pointed star.

Preparation:
Bend each toothpick in half so that it's almost broken but is still connected and it forms a narrow "V" shape. Arrange the five toothpicks in a circle on a hard surface with the bent centers inward as shown below.

Presentation:
Challenge a student to make a five-pointed star out of the broken toothpicks. This is easy enough; you could just turn all the toothpicks around. But can you do it without touching the toothpicks?

Place a few drops of water (not too much!) in the center of the toothpick arrangement, making sure that water is touching all of the toothpicks. Watch in amazement as the toothpicks slowly move to form a perfect five-pointed star. Try doing this on an overhead projector so everyone can see!

OVERHEAD VIEW

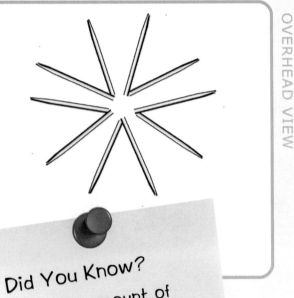

Did You Know?
The same amount of wood that it takes to make a single sheet of copy paper would yield 83 toothpicks.

4 + 4 = 6 PUZZLE

Objective:
Encourage problem-solving and creative thinking.

What's Seen:
You arrange six coins into two rows of four.

Materials Needed:
• Six quarters (or you can use buttons, poker chips, CDs, or other flat objects)

The Secret:

The secret of this challenge is so simple and sneaky that it's almost a trick question! You simply pick up the rightmost coin and place it on top of the center one.

Presentation:

Arrange the six coins in a cross on the tabletop as shown below.

Challenge students to figure out how to rearrange the quarters into two rows of four. If you wish, you can give them the hint that they only need to move one coin to accomplish it.

If no one solves it, show how easy and sneaky the challenge is by clearly moving the rightmost coin and placing it on top of the center one, making a plus sign. The two lines of coins share the two coins in the center to make "two rows of four."

Use this as one of a series of challenges or puzzles, maybe for a rainy day recess. You could give a prize or reward to the first person or team who solves the puzzle.

SNEAKY MOVE

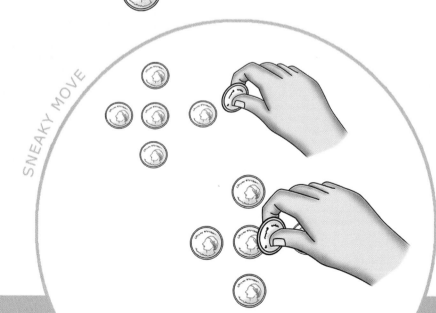

KIRIGAMI RING

Objective:
A fun reward or incentive for good work or behavior.

What's Seen:
You cut a hole in a 3" x 5" index card large enough to step through! Or challenge your students to guess how far apart the two dots can be spread.

Materials Needed:
- Index cards or copies of special Kirigami pattern
- Scissors

The Secret:

There is a special way of cutting up the index card so that it can expand into a really large ring. Once you know the series of cuts, you can use a regular index card with no markings, but when you first start it's a good idea to follow a pattern.

You can also try making fewer cuts and making them farther apart. The resulting ring won't be as large, but you'll get a feel for how to do it. Then progress to the full fifteen cuts. Practice this until you can do it quickly and neatly without tearing the card.

Preparation:

Use the Kirigami pattern below to draw cut-lines on a 3" by 5" index card. Or, you can download it directly from www.TeachByMagic.com/BOOK and print it out.

If you would like to do the challenge to see how far apart the dots can be spread while leaving the card in one piece, make two dots with a colored marker near the center of the index card as shown below.

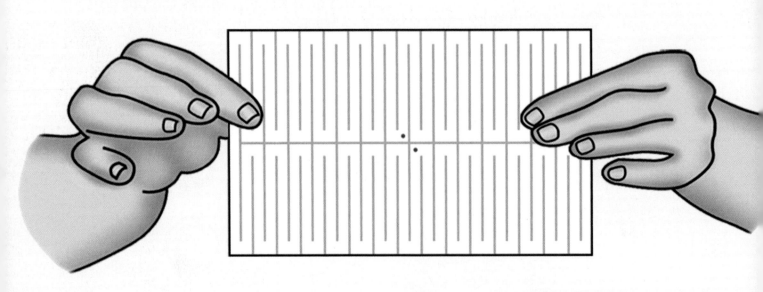

Presentation:

Issue the challenge by showing the card with the two dots. Ask students to guess how far you can spread the two dots from each other by cutting the card but keeping it in one piece. Alternatively, tell them you can spread the dots 30" apart while leaving the card in one piece and challenge them to find a way to accomplish the feat.

Maybe issue the challenge on Monday and give students until Friday morning to come up with a solution. Offer the demonstration of the answer as an incentive or reward for good behavior, homework completion, or whatever other goal you set.

To demonstrate the solution, fold the card in half lengthwise with the dots showing on the outside. Starting with the folded edge, cut fifteen slits equally spaced across the card; make each slit from the fold to 1/4" from the free edges.

Next, starting from the free edges, cut fourteen slits to within 1/4" of the fold. Make each slit halfway between two of the slits from the folded edge.

Finally, unfold the card and cut along the fold, leaving the two ends intact.

Now you're ready to gently (so you don't tear the paper) open and separate the cut strips to make a ring about 60" (five feet!) in circumference. This is big enough to put over your head and shoulders. You'll also be able to spread the two dots 30" apart!

Did You Know?

Kirigami is a variation of origami that includes cutting the paper.

The word comes from Japanese: "kiru," or to cut, and "kami," or paper.

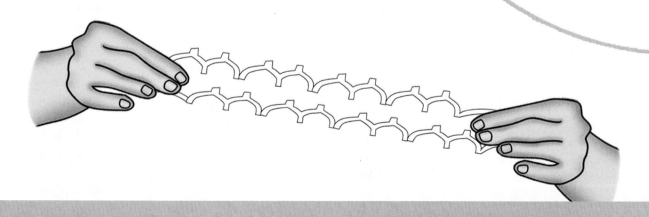

PAPER BRIDGE

Objective:
Encourage creative problem-solving or introduce concepts of physics.

What's Seen:
You can place a dollar bill over the space between two objects and balance a ceramic mug on it. You can even fill the mug!

Materials Needed:
- Dollar bill (a crisp one works best)
- Two cups
- Coins
- A mug

The Secret:

To make a flat sheet of paper stronger you need to add another dimension by folding, rolling, or even crumpling it up.

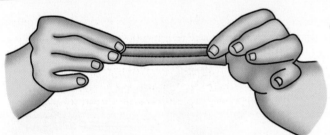

Presentation:

Show students the plastic cups and the dollar bill. Lay the bill on the cups and drop a penny onto the bill; the penny will fall. Give them their own cups and sheets of paper. Have them work in pairs or small groups. Challenge them to figure out how to create a bridge using only the paper (no tape, glue, or paperclips) that will hold up objects between the supporting cups. See whose bridge can hold the heaviest load (greatest number of pennies or other objects).

Rolling the paper allows it to support several pennies, and there are lots of ways to fold it to add strength. But the strongest paper bridge is made by folding the dollar accordion-style lengthwise. Such a bridge can support a mug full of coins!

Preparation:

There is no preparation other than gathering the needed items.

For this activity, you can use a whole sheet of paper instead of a dollar. This is easier and allows for larger bridges. Almost anything can be used for weights, such as pennies, rocks, toy cars, or erasers. Or you can use candy and let students keep as much as their bridges will hold.

AIR MAIL

Objective:
Challenge students to figure out how to keep a postcard from being blown off of a table without holding it or using any tape, glue, or weights.

What's Seen:
The postcard is easily blown off the table until you do the secret folds.

Materials Needed:
• Postcards

The Secret:

Folding the corners of a postcard allows air to flow under it, decreasing the air pressure beneath it and increasing the pressure above it, which holds it in place on the table.

Preparation:

Gather up old or inexpensive postcards. You can use super heavy cardstock but it must be really rigid; a standard index card isn't rigid enough.

Presentation:

Demonstrate that a regular postcard can easily be blown off a table. Invite a student to blow one off a desk.

Now challenge your students to figure out how to keep a postcard from being blown off of a table without holding it or using any tape or glue or sandbags or anything else. All they can do is fold the card. If you like, you can divide the class into groups and let them try different ways of folding it.

The secret folds to make a postcard as immovable as a brick are simple. Just fold down the four corners to make the postcard look like a little table with triangular legs. The triangles should be no larger than 1/2". If they're too big, the postcard can be moved by blowing on one of the triangles.

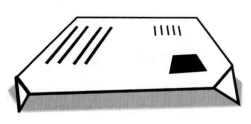

Did You Know?

"To Kill A Mockingbird" was the only book Harper Lee ever published.

She won a Pulitzer Prize for it.

ENGLISH

Amazing Spell-Checker

Review any spelling list with a magical stack of flash cards.

Magic Touch

Help students better comprehend what adjectives are by reviewing adjectives that have to do with the sense of touch in a fun and amazing way.

Remote Control Paper

Illustrate the difference between fiction and non-fiction with a piece of paper that moves when "pulled" by an imaginary string.

Word Warp

Review opposites or antonyms by showing a paper with a word printed on it that magically warps into the opposite word!

AMAZING SPELL-CHECKER

Objective:
Review the spelling of any set of words—for example, the numbers 1 through 10.

What's Seen:
You count through a stack of flash cards as you spell words. You know you spelled each one correctly because you always land on the card with that number or word.

Materials Needed:
- Thirteen special flash cards

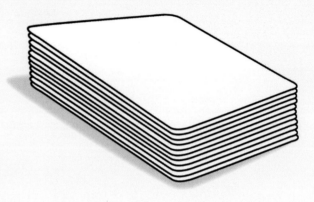

The Secret:

The cards are stacked in a special order. As long as the cards start in the correct order and you spell the words correctly, it will work every time.

SECRET STACK

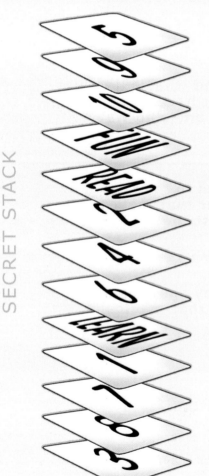

Preparation:

1. Print out the PDF for the sample set of words from www.TeachByMagic.com/BOOK or write the numbers and words yourself on note cards or cardstock. The suggested special words are READ, LEARN, and FUN.

2. If you like, you can laminate the cards or place them in baseball card sleeves.

3. Stack the cards in this order, with each card face-up: 3, 8, 7, 1, LEARN, 6, 4, 2, READ, FUN, 10, 9, 5.

When you turn the stack face-down, the top card will be the 3.

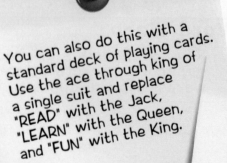

You can also do this with a standard deck of playing cards. Use the ace through king of a single suit and replace "READ" with the Jack, "LEARN" with the Queen, and "FUN" with the King.

Did You Know?

The first spell checker was developed in the late 1970s by a group of six linguists from Georgetown University for the IBM Corporation.

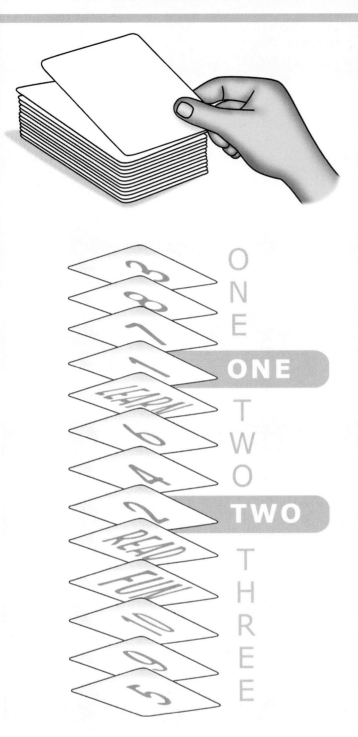

Presentation:

Announce that you are going to have a spelling review of the names of the numbers from one to ten. Show the stack of cards and explain that they'll be your spell-checker and will tell if you're correct or not.

Start with one: O-N-E. As you say each letter, move a card from the top of the stack to the bottom (holding the stack face-down). Say something like, "Do you think that's right? Let's see what the cards say." Turn the next card face-up, and it will be the number one.

Place the card face up on the table and continue in a similar manner for the rest of the numbers, each time setting the revealed card to the side. After the number ten, you will have just the three word cards left.

Say, "If you can spell, you can read." Spell the word READ while continuing to move the cards. Then turn up the READ card. Say, "If you can read, you can learn." Spell LEARN and turn up that card. Finally, show the last card and say that learning can be FUN!

You can use different words if you like. The word READ can be replaced with any word that has four or seven letters (so that the counting of the cards will come out correctly). LEARN can be replaced with any word that has an odd number of letters. FUN can be any word at all or even a picture.

PRACTICE ANY SPELLING LIST!!!

This trick is set up to do with number words mostly because it's fun to see the numbers show up in the correct order, but it can be done with any spelling words, big or small, and with any number of words.

All you have to do to create your own stacked order is go through the trick in reverse. Start with the last word on your list (no real counting there). Take the second to last word on your list and place it face-down on top of the first one. Then spell that word, taking a card from the bottom of your newly-created stack and placing it on top for each letter in the word. Now repeat for as many words as you have. As long as you remember the order of your spelling words, you're ready to go.

MAGIC TOUCH

Objective:
Help students better understand what adjectives are.

What's Seen:
You reach into a bowl and pull out a specific adjective without looking at it.

Materials Needed:
- Paper slip (roughly 11" by 4")
- Marker
- Bowl

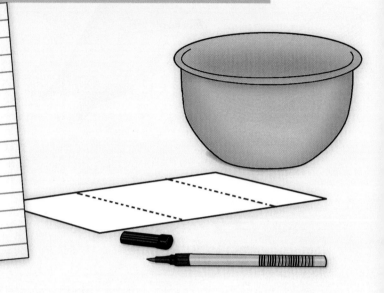

The Secret:

The word you are going to magically grab is always the second word written, so all you have to do is feel for the paper that has two torn edges because it came from the center slip of paper.

Preparation:

1. Cut the paper so that it's long and skinny. Make sure all the edges are cut smooth (not torn).

3. Draw two horizontal lines on the paper, dividing it into three equal sections.

Presentation:

Introduce the subject of adjectives and explain that an adjective is a word that describes the way something looks, smells, sounds, tastes, or feels. Ask students to name an adjective you can feel to describe some objects.

For example, a knife might be SHARP. Write that adjective in the first section of the paper (or have a student write it). Ask for another adjective describing how a different object might feel. Perhaps a puppy is SOFT. Write that adjective in the center section of the paper. Ask for a third adjective, for still another object. A frog is very SLIMY. Write that adjective in the third section of the paper.

CHOICE	PURPLE	HIDE
SLEEP	DIED	TIGER
ICE BOX	SQUARE	ECHO
TURTLE	COOKBOOK	LARGE
OBOE	ROSE	CHECK
WATER	DECIDE	TABLE

Hold the top of this page up against a mirror (the book should be at a right angle with the glass) and look at these words. Notice some can still be read and others can't. Can you figure out why? Go to www.TeachByMagic.com/BOOK to download a fun activity sheet that uses this concept to teach different parts of speech.

Have a student tear the paper along the lines and then put the three pieces into the bowl and mix them up. Now announce that you are going to reach into the bowl and pull out the adjective that feels soft (or whatever the second adjective was), using your "magic touch."

Have the student hold the bowl up or off to your side where you can't see into it, or turn your head or close your eyes. Reach into the bowl and feel the slips of paper. The second adjective, which was written in the center section of the paper, will have two torn edges. The other slips will only have one torn edge, so you can pull out the correct one every time.

Don't be afraid to take your time as you feel around—play it up and have fun with it. You might react to the "slimy" one or nick your finger on the "sharp" one for added effect.

REMOTE CONTROL PAPER

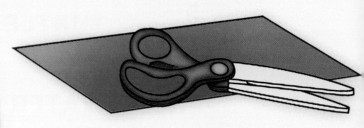

Objective:
Illustrate the difference between fiction and non-fiction.

What's Seen:
A piece of paper moves when "pulled" by an imaginary string.

Materials Needed:
- Scissors
- Small piece of paper (about 4" by 6")

The Secret:
There is a secret slit already cut in the paper that allows the paper to slide and bend. By pulling down on the paper with your thumb, the paper will bend over.

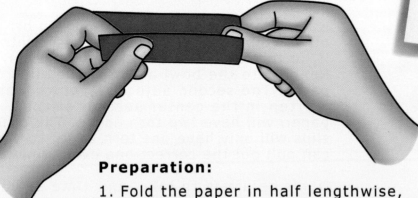

Did You Know?
The first TV remote control was invented in 1950.

It was called a "Lazy Bone," and it was connected to the TV with a wire.

Did You Know?
The word fiction comes from the Latin word "fictum," which means "created."

Preparation:

1. Fold the paper in half lengthwise, but only crease it about 1/3 of the way up from one end.

2. Cut a slit along the short crease you just made (remember, cut only 1/3 of the way up).

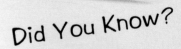

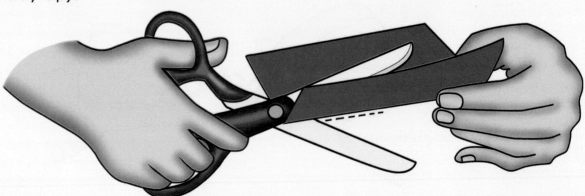

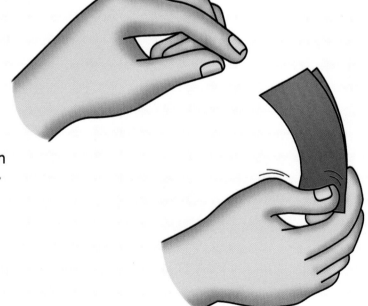

Presentation:

Explain that FICTION equals FAKE and FAKE equals FICTION. Have the class repeat that. Then say that NON-FICTION equals NON-FAKE, which is REAL. Show the piece of paper. It should be unfolded but held in your hand in such a way as to conceal the slit.

Announce that you're going to pull a hair from your head and use it, along with the paper, to show the difference between fiction and non-fiction.

Now fold the paper along the previous crease/slit. Pantomime pulling a hair from your head and wrapping it around the top of the paper.

Next, pantomime pulling the hair toward your body. As you do that, use your thumb to slide the paper so that it bends toward you as if it is being pulled by the imaginary hair.

Explain that you didn't really pull a hair from your head, that you just pretended to pull one out. The hair was fake; that was fiction. But the paper really did move; that was non-fiction. You may want to make the point that sometimes fiction can seem to be very real and that it's important to know how to tell the difference.

Also, just because fiction isn't real doesn't mean you can't learn from it. Many great works of literature show how people lived in different times and places and illustrate how they can learn and grow as they face life's challenges.

This is very easy to do and fun—try it! Just be careful not to let the students see your thumb moving.

It's a good idea to practice a few times beforehand to get the timing of the pantomimed pulling coordinated with the bending of the paper.

WORD WARP

Objective:
Review and reinforce the concept of opposites or antonyms.

What's Seen:
A piece of paper with a word printed on it is folded up. When it is unfolded, the word has warped or changed into the opposite of the first word!

Materials Needed:
• Copies of the special word warp words

The Secret:

There are two parts to the trick. The first is in the specially-provided words. These are called "ambigrams." They read as one word right-side up and a different word upside down (in this case, opposites). The second part is a tricky way of turning the paper upside down without it being obvious that you just flipped it over.

Preparation:

1. Make copies of the special Word Warp words in the back of this book. Or you can print these and many more Word Warp words with a downloadable PDF available at www.TeachByMagic.com/BOOK.

2. Pre-fold each paper. It's a good idea to have all the papers already creased along both folds to make it easier when you're doing it for real. This also allows you to practice a few times to make sure you know how to fold the paper to make it flip over.

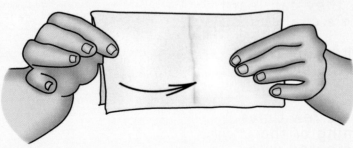

Presentation:

Explain the concept of opposites. Show one of the printed words and ask students what its opposite is. For example, EASY and HARD. Show the word EASY and announce that you're going to change it to its opposite by simply folding and unfolding the paper. With the word facing the class, fold the paper in half, lengthwise, so that the word is inside.

Next, keep the folded edge upward and fold the right edge across the front to the left edge.

Now unfold the paper in the reverse manner: open the back (nearest yourself) flap toward your right, then open the front (nearest the class) flap upward.

The paper will now be upside down from its previous position, and the word will have changed from EASY to HARD!

Bonus Lesson Ideas

The words used in this demonstration are ambigrams. An ambigram is a word or picture that appears to be one thing when viewed right-side up and something else when rotated upside down or viewed in a mirror. It's similar to an optical illusion. Ambigrams are also called vertical palindromes, designatures, or inversions. A very simple ambigram is the word "mom," which reads as "wow" when rotated upside down.

"Mom" and "wow" are also palindromes. A palindrome is a word or phrase which reads the same when the order of the letters is reversed. Other palindromes are the name "Anna" and the phrases "Step on no pets," and "Able was I ere I saw Elba."

Challenge your students to make lists of words and their opposites. At a higher level, challenge them to create palindromes and ambigrams or to find published examples of them.

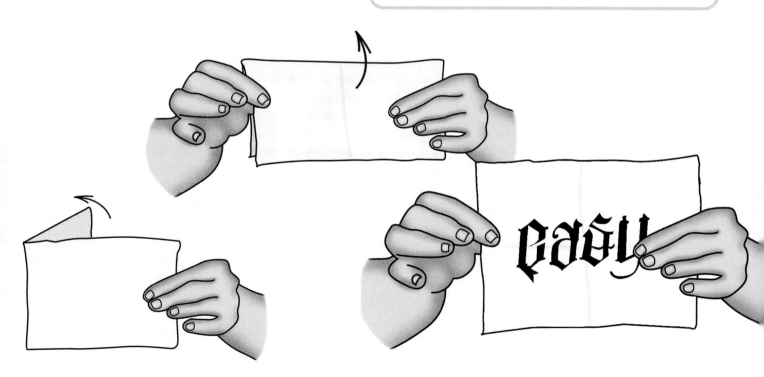

Did You Know?

In a classroom with 23 students, there is a 50% chance that two of them have the same birthday.

MATH

Karate Banana

Review basic math with a smart banana. Give the banana a math question and then peel it to discover the answer inside.

Adding Time

Read minds and predict the future with some simple math and the face of a clock.

Rectangle Squared

Review basic shapes and discover how a rectangle can turn into a square with the same area.

Calculator Cards

You can always guess which number a student has chosen, from one to sixty, using special calculator cards. Even more amazing is that it will make your students eager to practice basic addition.

Magic Moolah

Talk about fractions while you produce four quarters from a folded dollar bill.

KARATE BANANA

Objective:
Teach basic math skills in a visual and very memorable way.

What's Seen:
Bananas answer math questions! Ask the banana, "What is 6 - 2?" Then peel the banana to reveal that it is sliced into four pieces.

Materials Needed:
- Bananas
- Large pin or needle
- Plate or cutting board

The Secret:

The banana has been specially-prepared in a way that slices the banana with the banana peel still intact. Of course you know how many pieces you have sliced in each banana, so you can choose the one with the correct number to answer the question you ask. You could even make a tiny mark that only you will be able to see on each banana to help you remember its magic number.

Preparation:

Stick the pin into a banana and gently move it from side to side inside the peel. Be careful not to pierce the peel anywhere other than the original site. Repeat as many times as desired at different places on the banana. Hints:

1) Don't make all of the holes from the same direction or in a straight line.

2) Don't prepare the banana more than an hour ahead of performance time. If you prepare too far in advance the peel will dry out and the holes will become brown and be visible to the students. The browning can be minimized and delayed by rubbing a dab of lemon juice over the holes.

3) The trick is more dramatic if you leave the bananas joined in a bunch when preparing them and only separate them as you ask the questions.

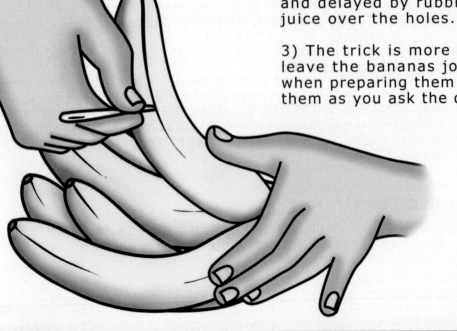

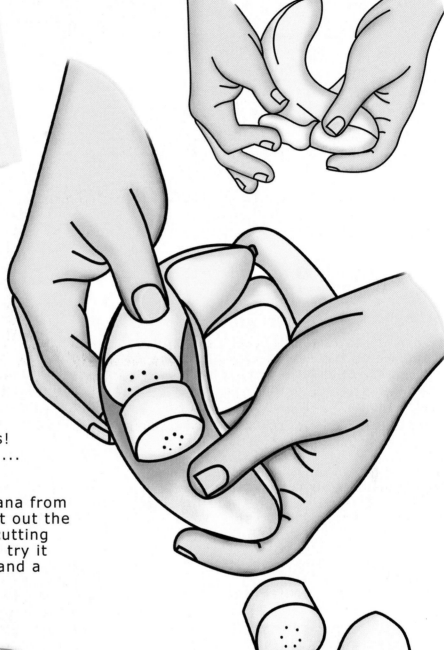

Presentation:

Announce that you have a bunch of the smartest bananas in town.

They are so smart they can answer math questions! Ask them a math question....

"What is 5 + 2?" Pull the appropriately prepared banana from the bunch and peel it. Count out the seven pieces onto a plate, cutting board, or paper towel. Then try it again with another banana and a different math problem.

Grandma's Banana Bread

2 1/2 cups flour
1 cup sugar
3 1/2 tsp. baking powder
1 tsp. salt
3 Tbsp. oil

3/4 cup milk
1 egg
1 cup mashed bananas
1 cup chopped walnuts (optional)

Preheat oven to 350° F. Grease and flour 1 large loaf pan or 2 small pans. Mix all ingredients together. Fill pans about 3/4 full. Bake 55-65 minutes. Let cool in pan, then remove and ENJOY!!!

Bonus Lesson Idea

For more advanced math, use the bananas to make banana bread and work on measuring and fractions.

Adding Time

Objective:
Review and reinforce basic math in a fun way.

What's Seen:
You can read minds and predict the future! A number is chosen from a clock face, a series of calculations are done, and then you miraculously know the results!

Materials Needed:
• Analog clock face

The Secret:

The difference between any number and its opposite on the clock face will always be six, so the calculations will all yield the same answer no matter which number is chosen.

Preparation:

This can be done with any clock face, but if you like you can print out a clock with arrows to make finding the opposite numbers easier at www.TeachByMagic.com/Book.

Presentation:

Show the clock face and ask each student to choose a number on the clock but not to tell anyone what it is. Then have them note the number directly opposite their chosen number on the clock face.

For example, if they chose 4, the opposite number would be 10. Now instruct them to subtract the smaller of the two numbers from the larger one. This result will always be 6.

Now have them do any series of calculations you choose, either mentally or on paper. For example, have them add 10 to that number, multiply that result by 2, and then subtract 8 from that.

Now tell them that you know what number they have as an answer. In this example, the answer is 24. To make the presentation more dramatic, plan in advance the calculations you will have the students do so you will know the answer. Make a show of writing it on a slip of paper and sealing it in an envelope before starting the presentation.

RECTANGLE SQUARED

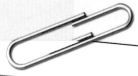

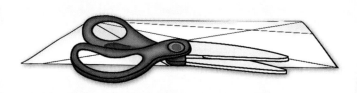

Objective:
Review basic shapes.

What's Seen:
Only two cuts are made in a 4" x 6" rectangle. The pieces are then rearranged to make a 5" x 5" square!

Materials Needed:
- Copies of the special rectangle
- Scissors

The Secret:

You just need to know which lines to cut and how to rearrange the pieces.

Preparation:

1. Make copies of the rectangle found in the back of the book or print it directly from www.TeachByMagic.com/BOOK.

2. Cut out the rectangle.

Presentation:

Show the rectangle and ask students if they think it's possible to cut the rectangle into some other shapes and then rearrange those shapes to make a perfect square.

Sure, you could cut it into a bunch of little 1" by 1" squares, but what if you were only allowed two cuts?

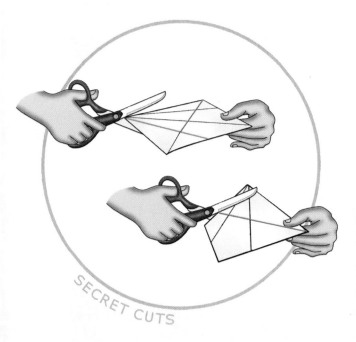

SECRET CUTS

Show your students the special rectangle to see if they can figure out which two lines you should cut in order to make three shapes that, when rearranged, form a square.

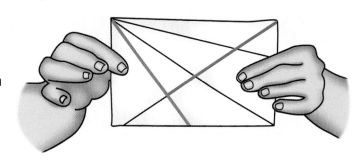

To demonstrate, the lines to cut have been colored. Cut the green line first, then the blue one. You now have two triangles and a four-sided polygon. For clarity, the pieces are shown here in different colors. First, arrange the pieces in the rectangle as they were before you cut them. Then rearrange them as shown below to make the square:

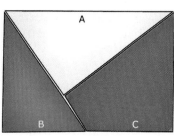

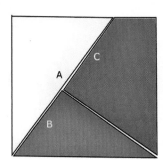

CALCULATOR CARDS

Objective:
Practice addition in a way that is so much fun, students will want to do it at home on their own.

What's Seen:
You can always guess which number a student has chosen, from one to sixty, by using special calculator cards.

Materials Needed:
- Copy of calculator cards
- Scissors

The Secret:

There is a key number in the upper left-hand corner of each card. Simply add together the key numbers from each card that contains the helper's chosen number, and the total will equal the chosen number every time.

Preparation:

1. Make copies of the calculator cards in the back of the book, or you can print them directly from www.TeachByMagic.com/BOOK. There are large cards to use for the class demonstration and smaller ones that you can print multiple copies of to hand out to the students.

2. Cut the cards apart.

3. If desired, laminate the cards for durability.

4. Put the cards in ascending order based on the number in the upper left corner of the card.

Lesson Idea

Teach the students how to use the cards and give each of them a set to take home so they can amaze their family and friends. They'll practice addition and have a lot of fun doing it!

Once they are comfortable adding the numbers with the cards in order from smallest to largest, have them mix the cards up to make it a little more difficult.

Did You Know?
The first mechanical calculator was invented in 1623, but it wasn't successfully produced commercially until nearly 200 years later.

Sum Puzzle

Can you make the following equation a correct statement by adding one single line to it? And in case you were wondering, the line does not go through the equal sign to make it "not equal."

$$5 + 5 + 5 + 5 = 555$$

Find the answer to this and lots of other fun puzzles at www.TeachByMagic.com.

Presentation:

Announce that it's time to practice addition. Explain that while now we usually use calculators, our parents and grandparents used calculator cards and did addition in their heads. Show the cards and ask a helper to choose a number between one and sixty.

Point out that some numbers appear more than once on the special calculator cards and you need to know how many times their number appears. (What you really need to know isn't how many times the number appears, but on which cards it appears.)

Show each card in turn and ask if the chosen number is on it. In your head, add together the numbers from the upper left-hand corner of each card that contains the student's chosen number.

After showing all of the cards, your result will be the chosen number. Make a show of mentally calculating the answer, then announce that the calculator cards have told you the number!

For example, if the number 24 is chosen, it isn't on the first card, or the second or third, but it is on the fourth card. That gives you 8. The number is also on the fifth card, so you add 8 to 16 and get 24. It's not on the sixth card, so you know the number is 24. Try it right now. Pick any number 1 through 60. It works every time.

01	11	21	31	41	51
03	13	23	33	43	53
05	15	25	35	45	55
07	17	27	37	47	57
09	19	29	39	49	59

(08)	13	26	31	44	57
09	14	27	40	45	58
10	15	28	41	46	59
11	24	29	42	47	60
12	25	30	43	56	

02	11	22	31	42	51
03	14	23	34	43	54
06	15	26	35	46	55
07	10	27	38	47	58
10	19	30	39	50	59

16	21	26	31	52	57
17	22	27	40	53	58
10	23	28	49	54	59
19	24	29	50	55	60
20	25	30	51	56	

04	13	22	31	44	53
05	14	23	36	45	54
06	15	28	37	46	55
07	20	29	38	47	60
12	21	30	39	52	

32	37	42	47	52	57
33	38	43	48	53	58
34	39	44	49	54	59
35	40	45	50	55	60
36	41	46	51	56	

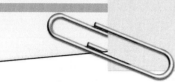

MAGIC MOOLAH

Objective:
Introduce the concept of fractions or a lesson dealing with money.

What's Seen:
You produce one or more quarters from a folded dollar bill.

Materials Needed:
• Dollar bill
• Four quarters

The Secret:

The quarters are behind the dollar bill between your thumb and index finger the entire time.

Preparation:

This just takes a bit of practice.

Presentation:

Announce that you are going to talk about fractions. Show the dollar bill and explain that it is the whole number "one." What your students don't know is you also have four quarters hidden behind the dollar, held between your fingers. Make sure they don't see the coins, but keep in mind they aren't looking for coins, so don't worry about it too much. Just act natural.

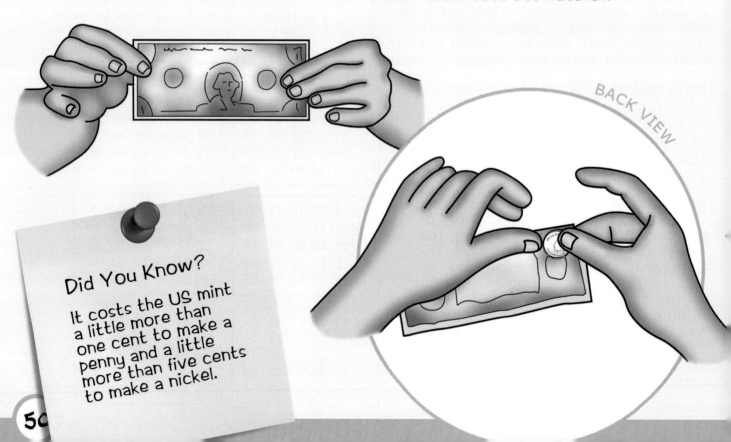

BACK VIEW

Did You Know?

It costs the US mint a little more than one cent to make a penny and a little more than five cents to make a nickel.

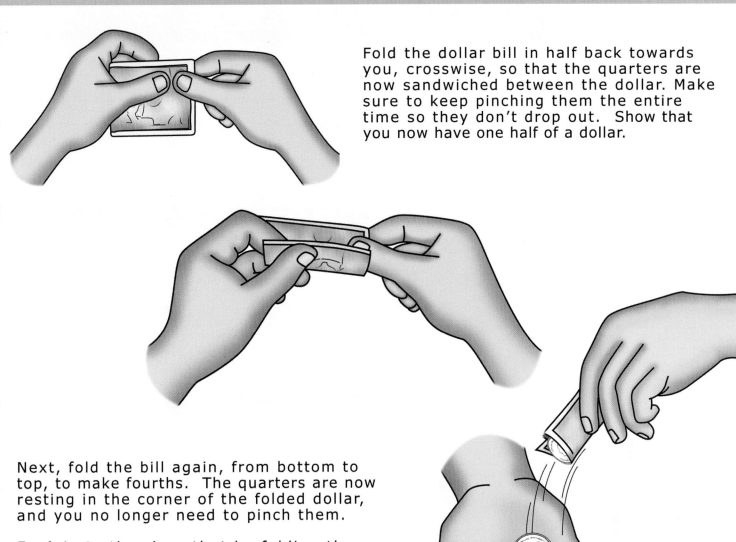

Fold the dollar bill in half back towards you, crosswise, so that the quarters are now sandwiched between the dollar. Make sure to keep pinching them the entire time so they don't drop out. Show that you now have one half of a dollar.

Next, fold the bill again, from bottom to top, to make fourths. The quarters are now resting in the corner of the folded dollar, and you no longer need to pinch them.

Explain to the class that by folding the dollar again, you created fourths, or quarters. Ask, "So how many quarters are in a dollar? That's right, four!" Then pour the quarters out of the folded bill.

Change the Trick...

Magic Moolah is also a great trick for teaching about making change. Do the trick with just one quarter behind the dollar bill. Ask the students, "If you buy a candy bar for seventy five cents and pay with a dollar, how much change will you get back?" Pour out the quarter to show they were correct. You could even have multiple dollars set up with a variety of coins and values for different purchases.

For even more ways to use Magic Moolah, visit www.TeachByMagic.com.

Did You Know?

The London bridge we sing about that keeps falling down isn't in England, it's in Arizona.

Because it was no longer structurally sound, it was dismantled in 1967, and the bricks were brought over and used to build a similar bridge in Lake Havasu City, Arizona.

Social Studies

Shortcut to Stardom

The legend of Betsy Ross is made more memorable by folding and cutting a single piece of paper and then unfolding it to reveal a perfect five-pointed star!

Never Wrong, Always Write

Your students will successfully guess which president they will be learning about without any hints.

20 Wonder Cards

Introduce a lesson on geography with a wonderful little card trick.

Bermuda Square

Get your students excited about geography, maps, and history with a puzzle where rafts appear and disappear off a map.

Objective:
Introduce the legend of how Betsy Ross created the first American flag.

What's Seen:
A piece of paper is folded, cut once, and then unfolded to reveal a perfect five-pointed star!

Materials Needed:
- Scissors
- Piece of standard copy paper

The Secret:

The only secret is the special way of folding the paper and knowing where to cut it.

Preparation:

Trim one inch from a sheet of paper to make it 8½" by 10". It's important that the paper be exactly the correct size for the star to look right.

Presentation:

Explain that Betsy Ross's grandchildren told the story of why the U.S. flag has five-pointed stars. Supposedly, George Washington thought that six-pointed stars should be used because five-pointed ones would be too difficult for seamstresses to make. Betsy then showed him this trick!

Did You Know?

Another way to make a star with one cut is to cut an apple crosswise through the core. This, too, will reveal a five-pointed star.

Fold the paper in half, so it is now 8½" by 5".

Fold it in half again, lengthwise, to make it 4¼" by 5".

Unfold it to the 8½" by 5" stage and make another fold, widthwise this time, so it is now 8½" by 2½".

Unfold it again to the 8½" by 5" stage. You will see the two crossed creases that you just made, as illustrated below.

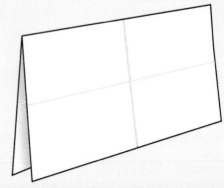

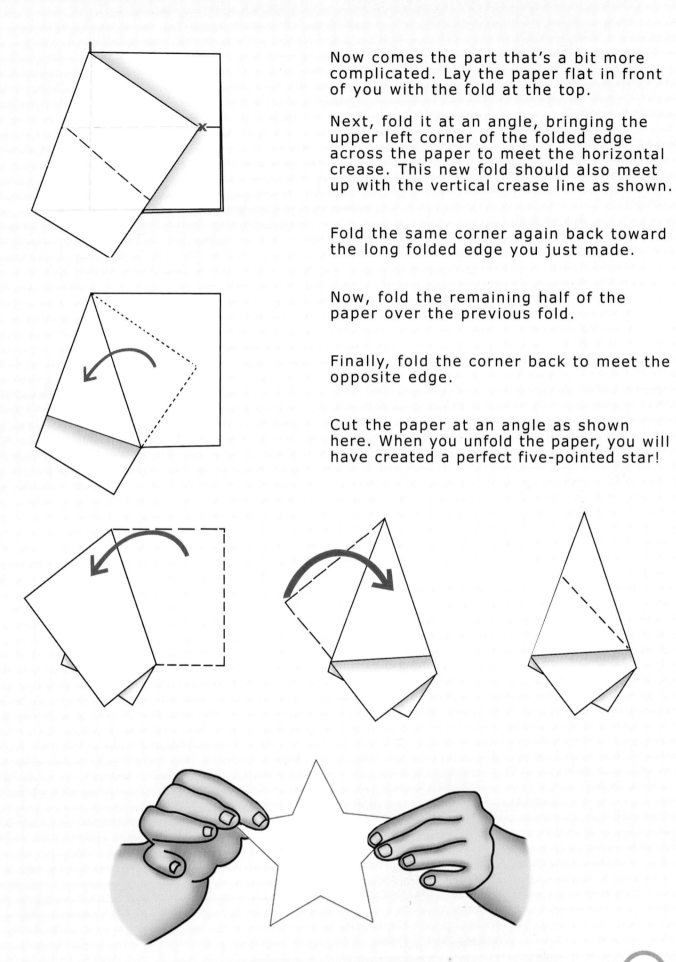

Now comes the part that's a bit more complicated. Lay the paper flat in front of you with the fold at the top.

Next, fold it at an angle, bringing the upper left corner of the folded edge across the paper to meet the horizontal crease. This new fold should also meet up with the vertical crease line as shown.

Fold the same corner again back toward the long folded edge you just made.

Now, fold the remaining half of the paper over the previous fold.

Finally, fold the corner back to meet the opposite edge.

Cut the paper at an angle as shown here. When you unfold the paper, you will have created a perfect five-pointed star!

NEVER WRONG, ALWAYS WRITE

Objective:
Introduce a lesson on one or more presidents of the United States.

What's Seen:
The class successfully guesses which president they will be learning about today.

Materials Needed:
- Photo of a president (or any item to represent your lesson)
- Marker
- Small slips of paper
- Bowl or small box

The Secret:

All of the slips of paper in the bowl have the same name or word written on them. As the students give names, they think you're writing the name they said, when really you're writing the same name over and over—the one you planned for the lesson! Just make sure you fold the sheets so nobody can see that they all say the same thing.

Preparation:

1. If you are not using slips of paper that are already about the right size (like from a little note pad), cut a piece of paper into little slips about 2" by 4". But really any size will work fine.

2. Place the lesson item in an envelope or gift box or, if it's in a picture frame, cover it or place it face-down.

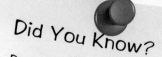

Did You Know?

Ronald Reagan was the 40th president of the United States, but there were only 38 before him: Cleveland was elected for two non-consecutive terms and is counted twice, as our 22nd and 24th president.

Presentation:

Challenge students to figure out which president will be the subject of today's lesson. Show them the picture frame (with the back of it toward them) and say that since they are such an amazing class you think they can work together and guess the president. Place the photo face-down and say that in a few minutes we will all find out if they guess right.

Ask students to name several presidents, and write on a slip of paper for each one. Of course, you aren't writing what they say; you write your lesson item or person every time. So in this example, every slip of paper will say Lincoln.

NOTE: Make sure you are far enough away that no one can see exactly what you are writing, but don't cover or hide it in any way as this will seem suspicious. If you act normal, the students will have no reason to doubt you are writing what they are saying.

Also, if the lesson item is a short word like the state "Maine," when someone says something longer like "Mississippi," take your time writing each letter so it is believable that you wrote the longer word.

Fold the written slip, drop it into the bowl, and then do another. Keep doing this for as long as you like. The more names you put in, the more amazing it seems. Plus, this is a great way to get your students thinking about all the different presidents.

IMPORTANT: You have to make sure someone says the item you are writing down. If no one ever says Abraham Lincoln, it would be suspicious, so just keep going until someone does.

After all the slips are written, have a student close her eyes and pick one from the bowl. Have her read the name on it and then show the photo. She was right!

You could take credit for predicting what they will choose, but it's a lot more fun to give the students credit for the incredible feat. Plus, when they ask how you did it, you can say, "I didn't do it. You did!"

Would you like to see something that has **NEVER** been seen before and that will never **be seen again** ?

Go to www.TeachByMagic.com and search for "Mystery Boxes." Look for George W. Carver and be prepared to learn a little more about a great American. Then you too can show your students an item that has NEVER been seen before and will never be seen again.

20 WONDER CARDS

Objective:
Introduce a lesson on geography (it can be states or countries).

What's Seen:
A student removes a few cards from the top of a stack and counts them as you lay out more. You count back the number of cards taken off, and the card you turn up will be the subject of the day's lesson.

Materials Needed:
- About 50 flash cards (states or countries)
- One or more objects to represent the lesson topic

The Secret:
The chosen card is pre-set as the twenty-first card from the top of the stack. (Get it? Twenty-one—twenty-wonder!)

The trick works mathematically. As long as your student removes fewer than 20 cards and you make sure you count accurately, it will work every time.

Presentation:
Show your box and announce that it contains a souvenir from your summer vacation. Ask for a student to help reveal where you went on that vacation.

Place the prepared deck of flash cards on the table and ask the student to remove a small number of them from the top and count them silently.

Preparation:
1. If you don't have state flash cards, you can download these and many more for other subjects at www.TeachByMagic.com and print and cut them out.

2. Count 20 cards from the top of your stack. Place the pre-selected (target) card on the stack. Put a small, unobtrusive mark on the back of the target card so you can tell which one it is in case of a counting error.

3. Put the 20 cards back. Your target card is now the 21st card from the top.

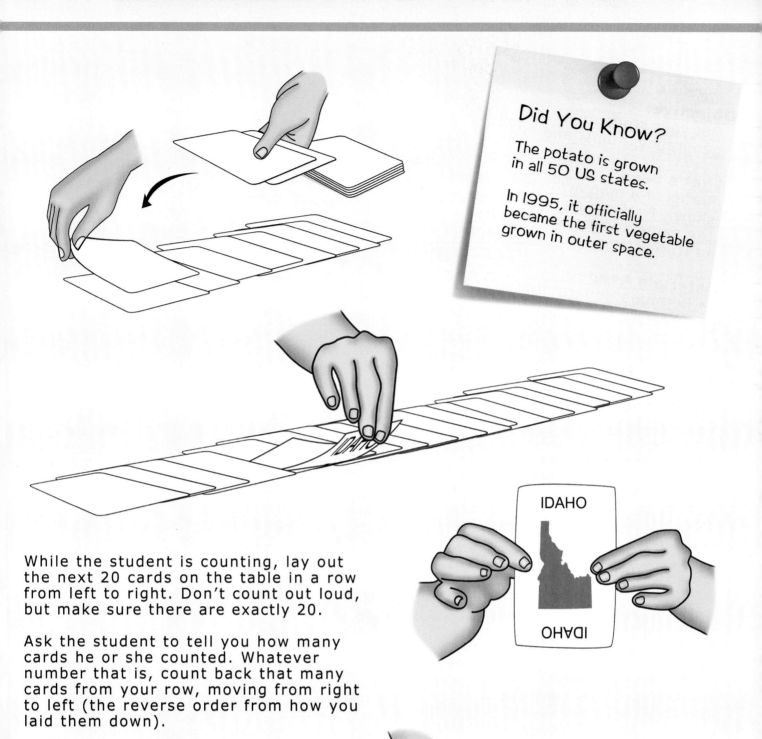

IDAHO

OHADI

While the student is counting, lay out the next 20 cards on the table in a row from left to right. Don't count out loud, but make sure there are exactly 20.

Ask the student to tell you how many cards he or she counted. Whatever number that is, count back that many cards from your row, moving from right to left (the reverse order from how you laid them down).

The last card you get to will be your pre-selected target card. Show it, then open the box to reveal the souvenir or symbolic objects. Alternatively, show the souvenir first and ask students to guess what it represents or where it's from before you show the card.

This is another trick where you could take the credit for predicting what they will choose, but it's better to give the students credit for the amazing feat. Plus, when they ask how you did it, you can say, "I don't know. How did you do it?"

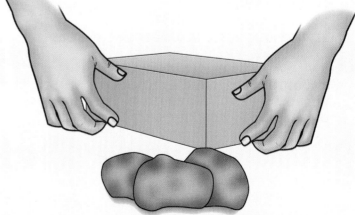

BERMUDA SQUARE

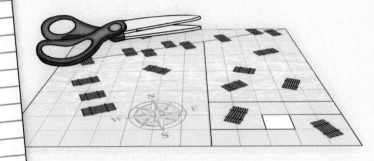

Objective:
Get your students excited about geography, maps, and history.

What's Seen:
Pieces of a map arranged one way show 21 rafts. Arranged differently in the same space, the map has a hole in it, and one raft has disappeared!

Materials Needed:
- Bermuda Square printout
- Scissors

The Secret:

There are logical explanations to how the raft disappears and a hole appears. It's a combination of two other popular puzzles. In the spirit of the Bermuda Triangle, we'll leave this one a mystery. (If you just can't handle not knowing, it's explained in detail at TeachByMagic.com.)

Preparation:

1. Make copies of the Bermuda Square in the back of the book, or you can print it out directly at www.TeachByMagic.com/BOOK.

NOTE: A larger version is also available at the site so you can put it up on the board. You could also copy the normal size to a transparency so the whole class can see it.

2. Cut out all the different pieces.

3. Review the explanation that accompanies the template or watch the video several times to make sure you understand how the paradox works.

Presentation:

Introduce the subject of the Bermuda Triangle and perhaps share some interesting facts and legends about it. Tell your students that you have found a map to the Bermuda Square and you think it might have some of the same mysterious characteristics as the Bermuda Triangle.

Start with the puzzle pieces arranged in the 12" by 12" grid so that there are 21 rafts.

Tell the class to carefully count the rafts and also count the squares on each side of the grid to verify that there are really 21 rafts and that the map is a perfect 12" by 12" square.

Have them watch closely as you rearrange the pieces to form the second configuration. Then have them count the rafts again. Now there are only 20! Plus, the grid is still 12" by 12", but one square is missing!

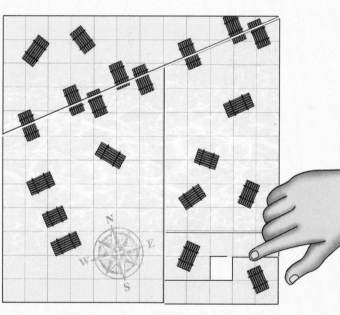

The Ballad of the Bermuda Triangle

(To the tune of "Gilligan's Island")

Just cut these out, and you'll see a trick,
A trick of a fateful place.
Where ships and planes all disappear
Without a single trace!

A triangle called Bermuda,
Where a total mystery
Has fascinated all mankind
Throughout history, throughout history!

The triangle is just a myth,
Or so the skeptics say.
But sailors make for a fearful crew
When they sail that way,
When they sail that way.

This magic trick will be the proof
That the triangle is real.
Just cut along
The darkened lines.
The pieces
Total four.
Arrange them in
A twelve-by-twelve
Grid on the floor.

Now all you do is count the rafts;
There should be twenty-one.
Then rearrange the pieces.
One goes missing, O what fun!

The size of the grid, it will not change.
It is always twelve-by-twelve.
Yet magically a hole appears!
Into this problem you should delve.

Down the hole that raft must go.
Where else could it be?
Unless it sailed to Bermuda....
It'll fool you, we guarantee!

So share this with your schoolroom class.
Every student will agree
It's tons of fun to try and solve
This Triangle Mystery!

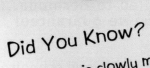

Did You Know?

The moon is slowly moving away from the earth. But don't worry—it's only about 3.8 centimeters a year.

SCIENCE

Skewered Balloon

Illustrate how a cell's membrane protects its contents by showing how a bamboo skewer can be passed through an inflated balloon without popping the balloon.

Wonder Bag

Show how chemical compounds are made by mixing pieces of paper representing sodium and chlorine in a paper bag and pouring out real table salt!

Instant Ice

Vividly illustrate the temperature at which water freezes to become ice by magically turning water into ice when it's poured into a cup with "32°" written on it.

Water Tower

Present physics concepts such as air pressure, fluid dynamics, and viscosity as water is moved from one glass to another without touching either glass.

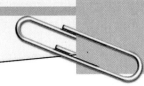

SKEWERED BALLOON

Objective:
Illustrate how a cell's membrane protects its contents.

What's Seen:
A bamboo skewer is passed through an inflated balloon, and the balloon doesn't pop!

Materials Needed:
- Bamboo skewers
- Large latex balloon
- Petroleum jelly

The Secret:

The balloon and skewer have petroleum jelly on them that acts as a seal to keep the balloon from popping.

Preparation:

1. Rub two skewers together along their lengths to smooth away any obvious splinters.

2. Coat one of the splinter-free skewers with a light film of petroleum jelly. Make sure there aren't any visible blobs.

3. Turn the balloon inside-out and put a dab of petroleum jelly inside it at the end opposite the mouth. Turn it right-side-out again.

4. Inflate the balloon and secure the end with a knot. Don't fully inflate it, though. You need to still be able to see and feel the small, thicker nub at the end of the balloon. If you over-inflate the balloon, the trick won't work. If desired, wait and inflate the balloon in front of the class as part of the presentation.

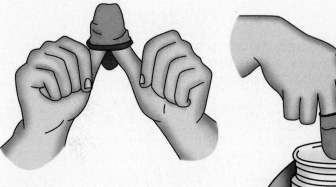

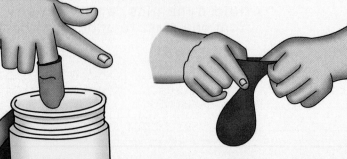

Presentation:

Begin by explaining that a cell's membrane protects its contents just as the balloon holds its air inside. Since the cell membrane is semi-permeable, it allows some things to pass through and keeps other things out. During this explanation, you are holding the balloon and feeling for the nub at the end.

Place one fingertip on the nub. When explaining permeability, poke the prepared skewer into the balloon just beside the knotted mouth (where the balloon is still thicker and stronger), and aim it at the fingertip that is over the nub.

Continue pushing the skewer through the balloon and all the way out at the nub, while holding the balloon sideways to the audience so they can't see the entry or exit sites.

When you get to the part about the membrane keeping some things out, pop the balloon with the skewer (this destroys the evidence; other-wise the balloon will slowly deflate).

Can You Believe Your Eyes?

Which Square Is Darker, X or Y?

A: Our interpretation of color is greatly influenced by surrounding colors. This is effect is called "color assimilation." Incredibly enough, the two shades of grey are exactly the same. Don't believe it? Punch two holes in a scrap piece of paper so you can cover everything except the X and Y squares.

Which Skewer Is Longer?

A: Vertical objects tend to appear longer than horizontal objects. The skewers here are actually the same length. Don't believe it? Grab a sheet of scrap paper and fold it to equal the length of either one.

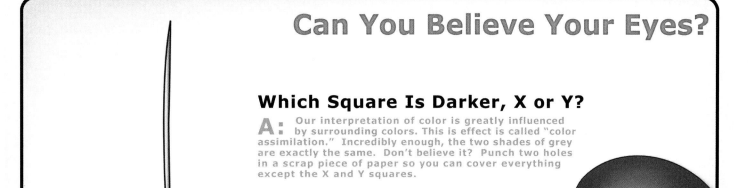

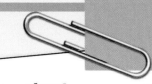

WONDER BAG

Objective:
Show how chemical compounds are made in a fun and visual way.

What's Seen:
Pieces of paper representing sodium and chlorine are mixed in a paper bag and real table salt is poured out!

Materials Needed:
- Two identical paper lunch bags
- Scissors
- Small papers and a marker
- A bowl
- Table salt

The Secret:

The Wonder Bag isn't just a paper lunch sack. It's a paper lunch sack with another paper lunch sack inside of it, creating a bag with two different compartments in it. This allows you to switch almost any two objects that will fit into the bags.

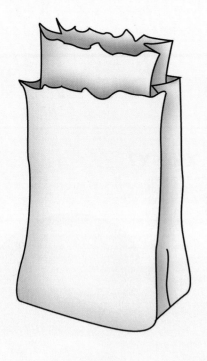

Preparation:

1. Trim off about half an inch from the mouth of one of the bags.

2. Insert the trimmed bag into the other bag. Make sure the folds at the bottom of the bags are aligned in the same direction so the outer bag can fold flat. For explanation purposes, we'll call the trimmed bag the "inner bag" and the space between the trimmed bag and the unaltered bag the "outer bag."

3. Pour about half a cup of table salt into the inner bag.

4. Prepare several cards or slips of paper about the size of business cards.

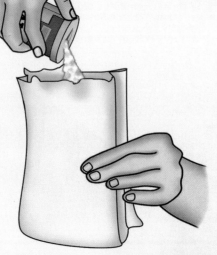

Presentation:

Show the bag and explain that it will create a chemical compound from two elements. Suggest that you will start with something simple, such as salt. Explain that salt is sodium chloride, a compound of sodium and chlorine. Write the symbol for sodium (Na) on a few cards and the symbol for chlorine (Cl) on the same number of cards, placing each card in the bowl as you do so.

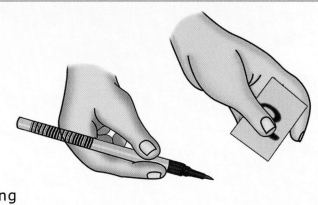

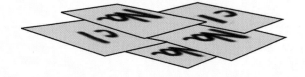

Open the bag to place the cards in the outer bag keeping the inner bag with the salt closed. NOTE: When opening the bag, hold the inner bag closed against the back of the outer bag and always keep the mouth of the bag away from the students so nobody can see the inner bag.

Explain that when the elements are placed in the bag they will combine to become salt. Then pour the cards from the bowl into the outer bag. Fold over the top of the bag to close it. If desired, shake the bag, blow on it, or say, "Chemistry is amazing!"

Finally, open the inner bag with both hands, holding it tightly against the outer bag so that none of the slips of paper can fall out, and pour the table salt into the bowl.

67

INSTANT ICE

Objective:
Vividly illustrate the temperature at which water freezes to become ice.

What's Seen:
Water is poured into a cup with "32°" written on it, and ice is immediately poured out.

Materials Needed:
- 8 opaque plastic cups
- Sponges
- Scissors
- Marker or printed labels
- Ice cubes and water

The Secret:

The cup with "32°" written on it is specially-prepared with a sponge and a few ice cubes. When the water is poured into the cup, it is absorbed by the sponge. The ice cubes that were already there can be poured out without the water, so it looks as if the water has turned into ice.

Preparation:

1. Label seven of the cups with the following temperatures (Fahrenheit): 44°, 41°, 38°, 35°, 32°, 29°, and 26°.

2. Cut one circle from the sponge that is the same diameter as the bottom of the cups. Cut another sponge circle that is slightly larger.

3. Soak the sponge circles and then squeeze out the water into the un-labeled cup. This is the water you will use for the demonstration, and, by doing this, you know the sponges can hold all the water.

4. Put the two sponge circles in the bottom of the cup labeled "32°"; put the smaller one in first and then the other one on top of it. Ideally, there should be a bit of space between them.

5. Put two ice cubes into the 32° cup on top of the sponges. Make sure the cubes are just slightly melted so they're shiny and won't stick to the sponge.

6. Arrange the cups in descending order by the temperature on the label so that the students read them from left to right.

Presentation:

Announce that you are going to determine the temperature at which water freezes to become ice. Indicate the row of cups labeled with different temperatures.

Ask, "Do you think the water will freeze at 44º?" Slowly (you want it to appear that there is more water than there actually is) pour the water from the unmarked cup into the 44º cup. Pick up the 44º cup and swirl the water around a little. Say something like, "No, it's still water. Let's try 41º."

Pour the water slowly from the 44º cup into the 41º cup and swirl again. Once again announce that it is still water. Continue pouring the water into each successive cup until you reach the 32º cup. When you swirl that cup, the students should be able to hear the ice cubes.

Pour the ice cubes out onto the table, tipping the cup completely to show that all the water is gone. Be sure that the mouth of the 32º cup is away from your students so nobody can see the sponges inside it. Announce that 32º is the temperature at which water freezes to become ice.

It may help to practice the trick a few times before performing it, especially to get a feel for how slowly to pour the water so it looks like there is more than there actually is and to determine how much time to give the sponges to soak up all the water.

WATER TOWER

Objective:
Present physics concepts such as air pressure, fluid dynamics, and viscosity.

What's Seen:
Water is moved from one glass to another without touching either glass.

Materials Needed:
- Three clear plastic cups
- Large bowl or sink with water
- Two #2 (hexagonal) pencils
- Tray to catch water overflow
- Drinking straw

Preparation:

1. Fill the bowl (or a sink) with water and, if you like, color the water with food coloring so it will be more visible during the demonstration.

2. Place one glass on the tray with the open end upward.

3. Lay the two pencils across the top of the glass.

4. Hold the two remaining glasses underwater in the bowl (or sink). Hold them sideways as they fill with water and press them together mouth-to-mouth so the water doesn't spill out, then stand them on the pencils.

5. Carefully slide the top glass over slightly so it hangs over the edge of the bottom glass just a bit. Air pressure will keep the water in the top glass.

The Secret:

One of the secrets is to use the straw. But the real secret is the setup of the glasses. The top glass is slightly off center so that air can be blown into the upside down glass, which will displace the water into the bottom glass.

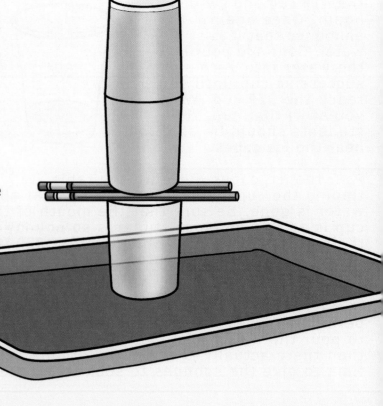

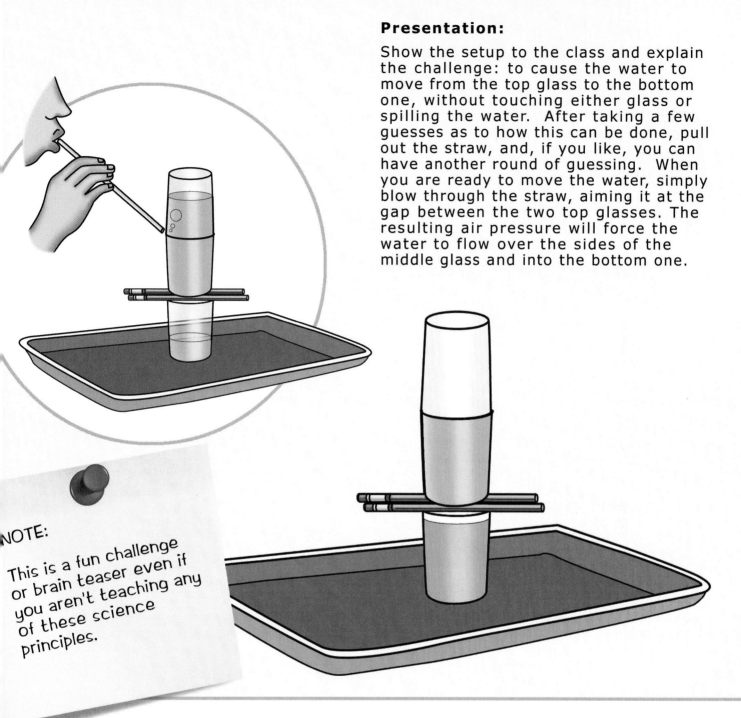

Presentation:

Show the setup to the class and explain the challenge: to cause the water to move from the top glass to the bottom one, without touching either glass or spilling the water. After taking a few guesses as to how this can be done, pull out the straw, and, if you like, you can have another round of guessing. When you are ready to move the water, simply blow through the straw, aiming it at the gap between the two top glasses. The resulting air pressure will force the water to flow over the sides of the middle glass and into the bottom one.

Bonus Lesson Idea

There are many ways to observe the movement and pressure of air and its effect on objects. Using the bowl (or sink) and one of the glasses from the above demonstration, you can show that air occupies space. Push an empty glass into the water upside down. The resistance you feel is air pressure! Now turn the glass sideways in the water and allow it to fill. Turn it upside down again and pull it upward, keeping its mouth underwater. You may feel slight resistance, and the water stays in the glass showing the effects of air pressure. Have several bowls or dishpans of water and many glasses so all of the students can try this.

Did You Know?

William Shakespeare never published any of his plays.

We have them today only because his fellow actors decided to record his work as a dedication to him.

FINE ARTS

Wonder Bottle

Make an arts and crafts project from recycled bottles. Then take a painted bottle and suspend it from a piece of rope.

Magic Number 9

Review the different families of musical instruments with an amazing card trick using instrument flash cards.

Eyes in My Fingertips

Introduce an art lesson on color by showing your ability to determine what color crayon you are holding without looking at it.

Mysterious Paper Bands

Learn about dimension in art by making and cutting different paper bands, each giving a different result!

WONDER BOTTLE

Objective:
Make an arts & crafts project from recycled materials.

What's Seen:
A painted bottle is suspended from a piece of rope.

Materials Needed:
- Empty plastic water bottles
- Paints and brushes
- Heavy string or twine (pipe cleaners or straws work as well)
- Small rubber ball (this can be made)

The Secret:
There is a secret ball hidden inside the bottle. This ball gets stuck and wedges itself between the neck of the bottle and the rope, allowing you to suspend, and even twirl, the bottle from the rope.

Preparation:
1. Use the paints to decorate your empty bottle any way you wish. The entire bottle needs to be covered so that the ball inside it can't be seen. Allow the paint to dry.

2. Cut your rope to be about a foot long.

3. Find or make a ball that barely fits into the mouth of the bottle you are using. Put the ball in your bottle.

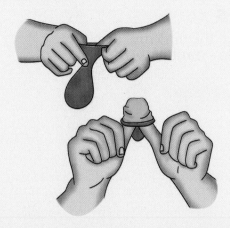

Presentation:
Show your finished bottle to the class, and explain that today's art project is also about recycling because you are going to re-use discarded items.

Explain that by painting this bottle, you have taken an ordinary bottle that could be taking up space in a landfill and turned it into a special "wonder bottle." Insert the rope and ask them to guess what will happen when you turn the wonder bottle upside down.

TWO WAYS TO MAKE A BALL

To make a ball out of a balloon, tuck the body of the balloon into the neck. Then twist the remaining tube and invert it back over the wadded balloon.

To make a ball using bath tissue, tightly wad a length of tissue and wrap rubber bands around it.

The finished ball should be small enough that you can squeeze it through the mouth of your bottle but big enough that it won't easily fall out or make noise when it bounces around.

Then do it. The ball will fall into the neck of the bottle, holding the rope in place so it doesn't fall out. Next, pull the rope down a little, slowly and gently, to firmly wedge the ball and the rope together in the neck of the bottle. Now you can hold the rope and drop the bottle. You can even swing the bottle around by the rope.

Have each student bring a bottle from home or provide one for them all. Distribute bottles, paints, and brushes to each student, and allow them to decorate their own bottles in any way they wish. There is no wrong way to paint a bottle. Once they are all dry you can show the students how to do the trick and give them each a small piece of rope and a ball (or the materials to make a ball).

While the students are decorating their bottles you can lead a discussion on recycling: other ways to re-use bottles, other items that can be recycled, and ways to do it. If your community has specific regulations on what can or cannot be recycled, or how to recycle particular items (sorting vs. commingling), you could talk about those or ask students to research that for a follow-up lesson.

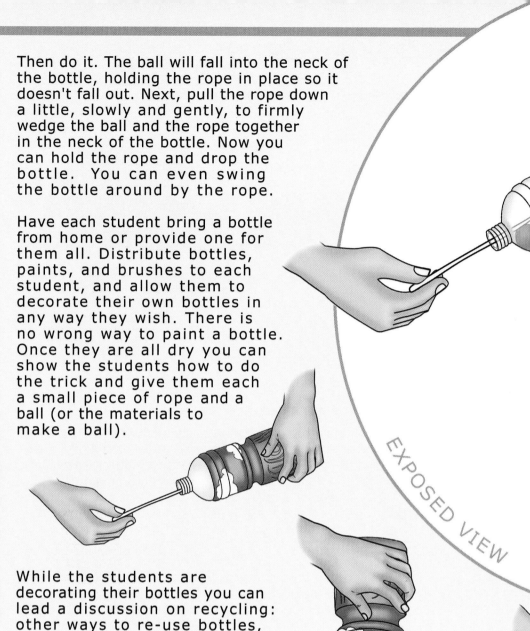

EXPOSED VIEW

Did You Know?

Americans buy an estimated 29.8 billion plastic water bottles every year.

Nearly 8 out of 10 bottles will end up in a landfill.

MAGIC NUMBER 9

Objective:
Review the different families of musical instruments.

What's Seen:
A number is selected that leads you to a random card. The instrument on that card is not only from the brass section, as predicted, but it matches the instrument you have in the case.

Materials Needed:
- 20 musical instrument flash cards
- An instrument in its case

The Secret:

Take any of the numbers between ten and twenty. When the sum of the two digits is subtracted from the original number, the result will always be nine. Therefore, moving the cards as described in the presentation will always leave nine cards on the table with your target card on top.

11	1 + 1 = 2	11 - 2 = 9
12	1 + 2 = 3	12 - 3 = 9
13	1 + 3 = 4	13 - 4 = 9
14	1 + 4 = 5	14 - 5 = 9
15	1 + 5 = 6	15 - 6 = 9
16	1 + 6 = 7	16 - 7 = 9
17	1 + 7 = 8	17 - 8 = 9
18	1 + 8 = 9	18 - 9 = 9
19	1 + 9 = 10	19 - 10 = 9

Preparation:

1. If you don't have cards with different instruments on them, you can print out the PDF from www.TeachByMagic.com/BOOK.

2. Put a small mark on the back of the target card so you can always tell which one it is in case of a counting error.

2. Count eight cards from the top of your stack, place the designated (target) card on the stack, then put the eight cards back. Your target card is now the ninth card from the top.

Presentation:

Announce that you're going to learn about musical instruments. Explain the different families and show a picture card representing each one.

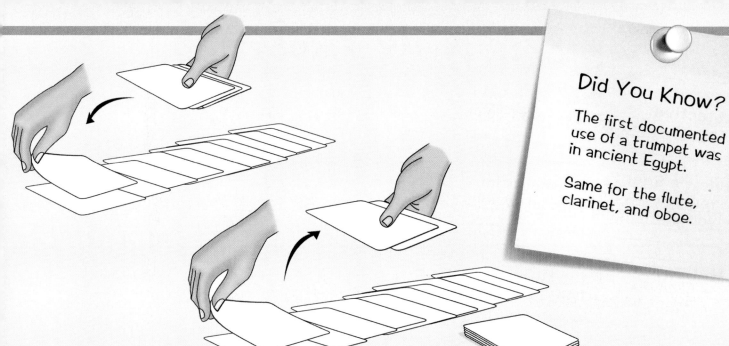

Did You Know?

The first documented use of a trumpet was in ancient Egypt.

Same for the flute, clarinet, and oboe.

Show a few more cards and place each one in its proper category. Now put all of the cards back on top of the stack. NOTE: All of these cards should have come from the top eight cards so that your target card remains the ninth card down.

Explain that you are going to randomly pick a flash card and see if you can get one from the brass section. Ask a student to choose a number between ten and twenty then add the two digits of that number together. That is how you will pick a card.

Ask them to tell you the original number, and count out that many cards onto the table, laying them from left to right, face down. Now ask them to tell you the result of the addition.

Pick up that number of cards, from right to left. The next card will be the target card or, in the example, the trumpet.

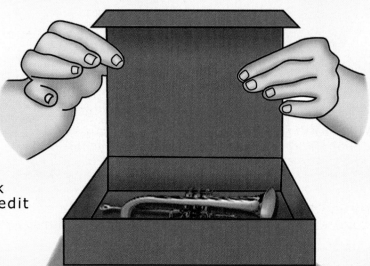

Amazingly, not only has your student selected a brass instrument, they picked the exact same instrument that is in the case.

This is a perfect example of a trick where you can give the student credit for making it happen and deny knowing how it was done. After all, Bobby did it!

EYES IN MY FINGERTIPS

Objective:
Introduce an art lesson on color.

What's Seen:
You can determine what color crayon you are holding without looking at it.

Materials Needed:
- Crayons
- Paper bag or box

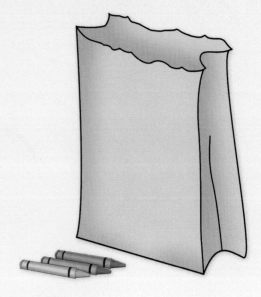

The Secret:

While you have the crayon behind your back, you scrape a bit of it with your fingernail. When you then bring that hand to the front to show the "eyes in your fingertips," you can see the bit of crayon under your fingernail and tell which crayon you picked.

Presentation:

Begin by explaining that our eyes can distinguish colors by means of receptor cells called cones. There are three types of cones: red-orange, green, and blue-violet. All other colors are seen as different combinations of those three.

Show the crayons, separating the three specific ones from the rest (or you can do this with as many different colors as you like to make it "more difficult").

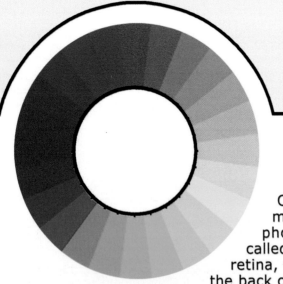

It's All In Your Head!

Our eyes perceive color by means of specialized photoreceptor cells, called cones, in the retina, which is at the back of the eye.

We have three types of cones: red, green, and blue. Note that these do not match the three primary colors! The three types of cones work together to detect the specific wavelengths of light reflected by any object. A region of the brain called the optical cortex then interprets the information provided by the cones to give the color a name such as green or yellow or purple.

Lesson Idea!

Using red, blue, and yellow paint, try mixing different combinations to see what colors you get. Have students try to create a color spectrum like the one above, using only the three primary colors of paint.

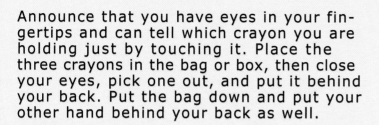

Announce that you have eyes in your fingertips and can tell which crayon you are holding just by touching it. Place the three crayons in the bag or box, then close your eyes, pick one out, and put it behind your back. Put the bag down and put your other hand behind your back as well.

Now scrape a little of the chosen crayon onto your fingernail and, as you do, say, "If I could see this crayon, the cones in my eyes would tell me what color it is; but I have eyes in my fingertips."

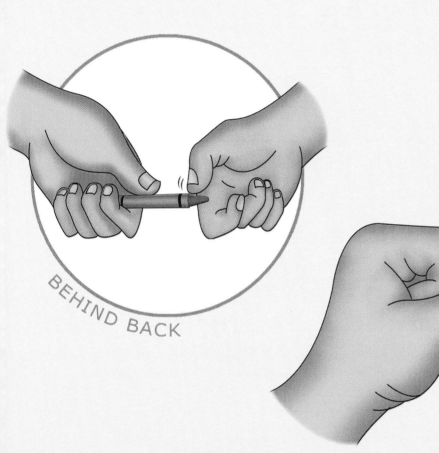

BEHIND BACK

Now bring the hand with the crayon shavings on it around in front of you, leaving the crayon behind in your other hand. Point your fingers at the students to let them see where your "eyes" are, while holding your thumb up to sneak a glance at the color on your fingernail.

Finally, announce, "My fingertips have told me that I picked the RED crayon." Bring the crayon around to your front and show that you are correct. Show the bag with the other two crayons still in it or dump them out onto the tabletop.

MYSTERIOUS PAPER BANDS

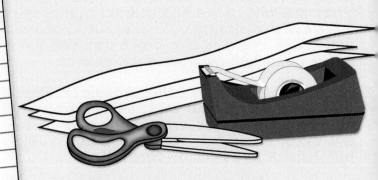

Objective:
Learn about dimension in art.

What's Seen:
A longitudinal cut is made in three paper bands, each giving a different result!

Materials Needed:
- Newspaper
- Scissors
- Tape or glue

The Secret:

You get different results from cutting each paper band because they are each twisted differently.

Preparation:

1. Cut three strips of newsprint about 2" wide by the length of the sheet.

2. Prepare the first strip by taping the two ends together to form a flat loop. Put tape on both sides of the band. Join A to C and B to D.

3. Prepare the second band by making a half-twist in the strip, joining A to D and B to C. Notice this strip has only one continuous side. This is called a Möbius strip.

4. Prepare the third band by making two half-twists (one full twist) in the strip, again joining A to C and B to D.

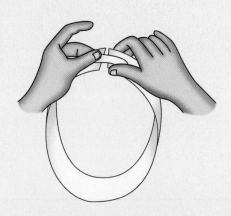

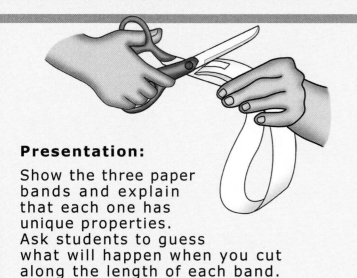

Presentation:

Show the three paper bands and explain that each one has unique properties. Ask students to guess what will happen when you cut along the length of each band.

Cut each band by folding it gently so that you can begin the cut along the center, as shown above. Then open the strip and insert the scissors. Cut down the middle of the strip, flattening out the twisted segment, until the cut is complete.

Strip 1 will become two separate bands.

 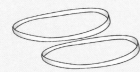

Strip 2, the Möbius strip, will become one larger band that is no longer a Möbius strip.

Strip 3 will become two linked bands, each with a full twist.

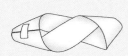 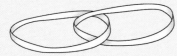

Primitive art was very two-dimensional. Cave paintings show people and animals in crude profile with single color pigments.

Later, Egyptian, Greek, and Roman cultures expanded their palettes of color and materials, but art continued to be confined to flat representations.

Medieval artists began experimenting with scale, which added the idea of "distance" within a two-dimensional space.

Finally, artists began to understand how to depict objects and scenes more realistically. By the Renaissance, art was full of form and perspective and depth.

Then nothing changed for centuries, at least in the sense of dimensionality. There were no attempts to go beyond the techniques of light and shadow and perspective in showing the world through art until the modern era. Artists like Picasso and Dali did, at last, begin to show the world through different arrangements of depth, perspective, and form.

M. C. Escher, however, was the first artist who really explored ways of going beyond three dimensions in a two-dimensional world. By playing with perspective, he created works that seemed to show water from a waterfall flowing back uphill only to fall again in an endless cycle. Or a room full of many stairways at different angles, where the law of gravity seemed to no longer be in force. His two-dimensional worlds were places that couldn't possibly exist in three dimensions.

Escher also created objects that could be manipulated to turn inside out or loops of paper that had only one side instead of two. And that's where these paper bands come in.

Did You Know?

The reason honey is so easy to digest is because it has already been digested by a bee.

HEALTH

Balancing Card

Find out what foods are part of a balanced diet by literally balancing them on a nutritional facts card.

Newspaper Tree

Emphasize the importance of recycling by making a large tree out of a roll of newspaper just by tearing it.

Rope Escape

Illustrate the importance of exercising and get some exercise yourself when you demonstrate how to remove a loop of rope that is trapped on another rope tied to your hands.

Linking Paperclips

Magically link two paperclips to show how easy it can be to get tangled in an addiction.

BALANCING CARD

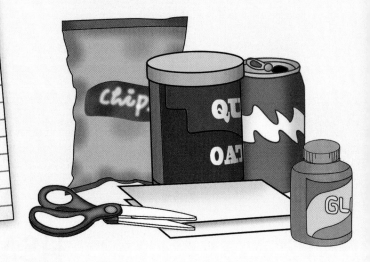

Objective:
Learn how to find out if a food item is part of a balanced diet.

What's Seen:
Foods that are healthy actually balance on top of a Nutritional Facts card. Unhealthy foods don't!

Materials Needed:
- Copy of Nutritional Facts image
- Cardstock
- Scissors
- Glue or double-sided tape
- Various empty food packages

The Secret:

There is a second card glued to the back of the Nutritional Facts card that acts as a flap. You control the position of the folded flap with your thumb.

Simply hold it flat for "unbalanced" items or move the flap out to support the "balanced" ones.

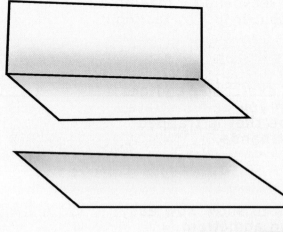

Preparation:

1. Make a copy of the Nutritional Facts card in the back of the book or print it at www.TeachByMagic.com/BOOK.

2. Glue or tape the facts card to some heavy cardstock and cut it to the right size.

3. Cut a second piece of cardstock the exact same size.

4. Fold the blank cardstock in half lengthwise.

5. Glue or tape one side of the folded cardstock to the back of the Nutrition Facts panel; align the edges carefully. This will create your secret flap.

6. If using glue, allow to dry thoroughly.

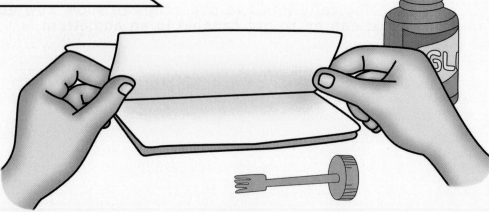

Bonus Lesson Idea

Ask students to collect and bring in clean, empty packages from various foods. Have them compare the Nutrition Facts from each one. Place healthy items in a box or basket (perhaps a picnic-type basket) and the unhealthy ones in the trash can (or recycling bin, depending on the item).

Presentation:

Introduce the concept of a balanced diet and healthy vs. unhealthy foods. Show the prepared Nutrition Facts panel and explain how it gives you the information you need to make healthy food choices. Show the various empty food packages and say something like, "Let's find out which of these foods are part of a balanced diet. If it is, it will balance on the edge of this card. If it's not part of a balanced diet, it will fall off." When trying an unbalanced food, hold the card so that the folded flap is flat against the front card. Make a show of trying to balance the item on the flat card, then let go and allow it to fall to the tabletop.

For items that are part of a healthy, balanced diet, fold the flap outward so it is at a right angle to the front card. The item can then "balance" on the T-shape that it forms.

Be careful how you hold the card so the students can't see the second card on the back. And remember, play up trying to balance all the items as that will distract attention away from the movement of your thumb adjusting the flap. As always, it's a good idea to practice a few times to get the timing and coordination right.

SIDE VIEW

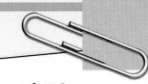

NEWSPAPER TREE

Objective:
Emphasize the importance of recycling.

What's Seen:
A roll of newspaper turns into a 5-foot tree.

Materials Needed:
- Newspaper
- Scissors
- Tape or a rubber band

The Secret:

The newspaper is rolled a special way and pre-cut so that it can easily be extended into a tree.

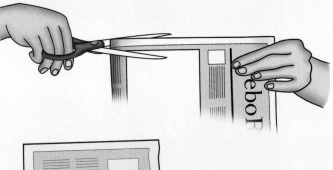

Preparation:

1. Trim off the folded edge of a section of newspaper to create several single-page sheets.

2. Begin rolling the first sheet into a tube about the size of a paper towel tube. Don't make your roll too tight or the tree won't "grow." When you get to about the last 8", tuck in the edge of the next sheet and continue rolling. Continue rolling in this manner until all sheets (at least 6) have been rolled. Stop rolling when you have about 8" left of the final sheet.

3. Using the scissors, make four cuts about halfway down the roll as shown below.

4. Roll the remaining 8" of paper around the slits and fasten with tape.

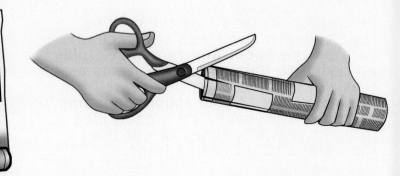

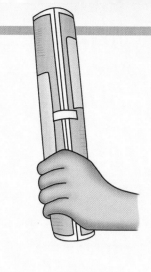

Presentation:

Benjamin Franklin said, "A penny saved is a penny earned." If he were talking about recycling, he would say, "A TREE saved is a TREE earned!"

So how do we save trees? We recycle!

Explain that paper comes from trees, but can trees come from paper? Well, yes. If we recycle our used paper, then we can save other trees from being cut down, so, "A tree saved *really is* a tree earned!" As you explain this, tear down the outer layer of the roll along the secret slits you made, like peeling a banana. Fold the strips outward just a bit to give them some spring, then pinch the strips in the center of the roll and pull them up and out to make a tree.

Here are a few creative ways to recycle newspaper:

1. Shred it (just the black and white pages) and add it to your compost pile.

2. Use it in crafts to make papier maché.

3. Use it for washing windows (it's great for removing streaks).

4. Use it as a drop cloth when doing messy tasks like painting.

5. Use the colored comic pages as wrapping paper for gifts.

6. Roll it tight and use it as a firestarter.

7. Crumple it up and use it as packing material when shipping things.

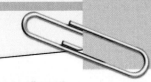

ROPE ESCAPE

Objective:
Illustrate the importance of exercising to get rid of unwanted body fat.

What's Seen:
A loop of rope is trapped on another rope tied to both of your hands. Can you get the rope off your body?

Materials Needed:
• Two six-foot lengths of rope (ideally, they should be two different colors)

The Secret:

The secret is simple but can take a while to figure out if you don't know it. The rope loop is placed over one arm and pulled through the little loop of the other rope that is around the wrist.

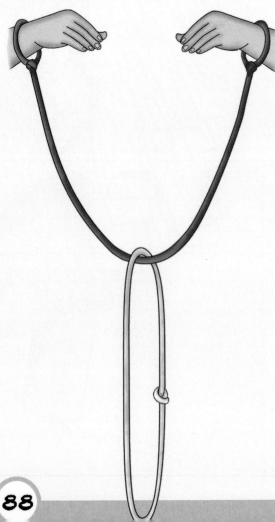

Preparation:

1. Secure the ends of each rope with tape or glue.

2. Tie a little loop on each end of one of the ropes. They should be big enough to slip around your students' wrists comfortably, but make sure they're not too big.

3. Tie the other rope into one big loop.

Presentation:

You can either choose one student to demonstrate this in front of the class or, ideally, you can prepare a few sets of ropes and divide the class into groups, giving everyone a chance to try to figure it out.

To set up the challenge, place one of the little loops in the first rope on one of your student's wrists. Now place the other rope, the one that is tied into one big loop, onto the first rope so that the first rope is threaded through the second rope as shown. Finally, place the other little loop on the other wrist so that the big loop is trapped on the student's body.

Explain to the class that the big loop of rope represents body fat and that fat slows us down just like these ropes. Ask the class if anyone knows of a good way to get rid of body fat.

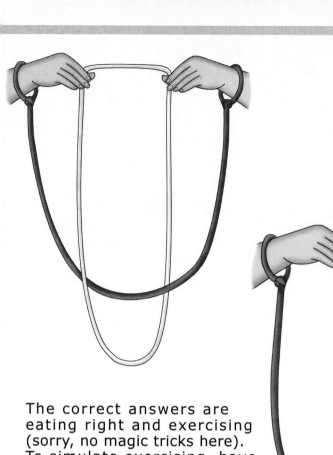

The correct answers are eating right and exercising (sorry, no magic tricks here). To simulate exercising, have the student step through the rope and maneuver it around their body a few different ways to try to get it off.

Most of the time it will take a while to figure out how to get the rope off, but it's the same principle with exercising. You can't just do a few jumping jacks and be done. You have to stick with it and eventually the fat will melt away.

If you have a student that doesn't figure it out on their own, help them by placing the big loop of rope on their left arm. Then have them grab the rope with their right hand and pull it through the little wrist loop. Suddenly, they are free!!!

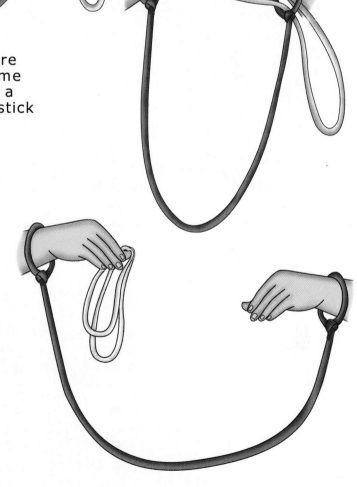

Double the lesson ideas...

You can double the fun! Instead of the loop of rope, you can have two students tied to each other with ropes on each wrist. This is even trickier to get out of and is a fun way to teach teamwork, problem-solving, or even evaporation. For information on how to do this visit www.TeachByMagic.com and search for the Double Rope Escape!

LINKING PAPERCLIPS

Objective:
Show how easy it can be to get tangled in an addiction, like drugs, if we hang around others that do drugs.

What's Seen:
Two paperclips are placed separately on a dollar. Then, when you pull on the ends, the clips fly off of the dollar and are linked together.

Materials Needed:
- Two large paperclips
- Dollar bill or piece of paper

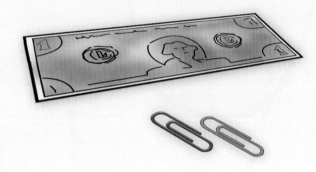

The Secret:

The secret is in the placement of the paperclips on the folded dollar bill.

Presentation:

Explain that today we are talking about drugs (the topic could also be smoking or drinking). Show the dollar bill and say, "In this example, this dollar will represent a party.

"Now you know there will be people there that use drugs, but you don't want to be left out of the party, so you decide to go anyway. You'll just stay away from the drugs, of course."

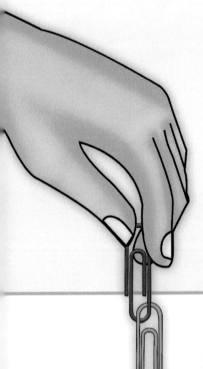

Stretching the Trick!

If you wish, you can add a rubber band to this trick:

A) Loop the band so it hangs around the center of the paper before folding. As you fold, keep the band between the two paperclips. The clips will link onto the band and hang from the dollar.

B) Place the band around the paper after the first fold and after placing the first clip. Again, keep it between the two clips. This time the clips will link to the band, and the band will fall off the bill with the paperclips.

Fold the dollar bill one third of the way over and place the first paperclip as shown here.

"This paperclip represents you."

Now fold the other third of the dollar back over and place another paperclip on as shown here.

"This paperclip represents another person at the party, who does drugs."

"Notice how the two paperclips are not even touching. But if you stay at that party long enough and hang around those types of people, you will eventually get caught up in their bad choices."

Pull on the two ends of the dollar bill, and the clips will come together, link, and fly off. Pick up the linked paper clips and show your students how quickly and easily it happened. Explain the importance of staying far, far away from anything that harms our bodies.

TIPS:

1) When tugging on the paper to link the clips, aim down toward the tabletop. Otherwise, the clips might fly out of reach or land on the floor.

2) The trick will be easier to see if you use colored paperclips.

3) When folding the paper, don't crease it, just bend it.

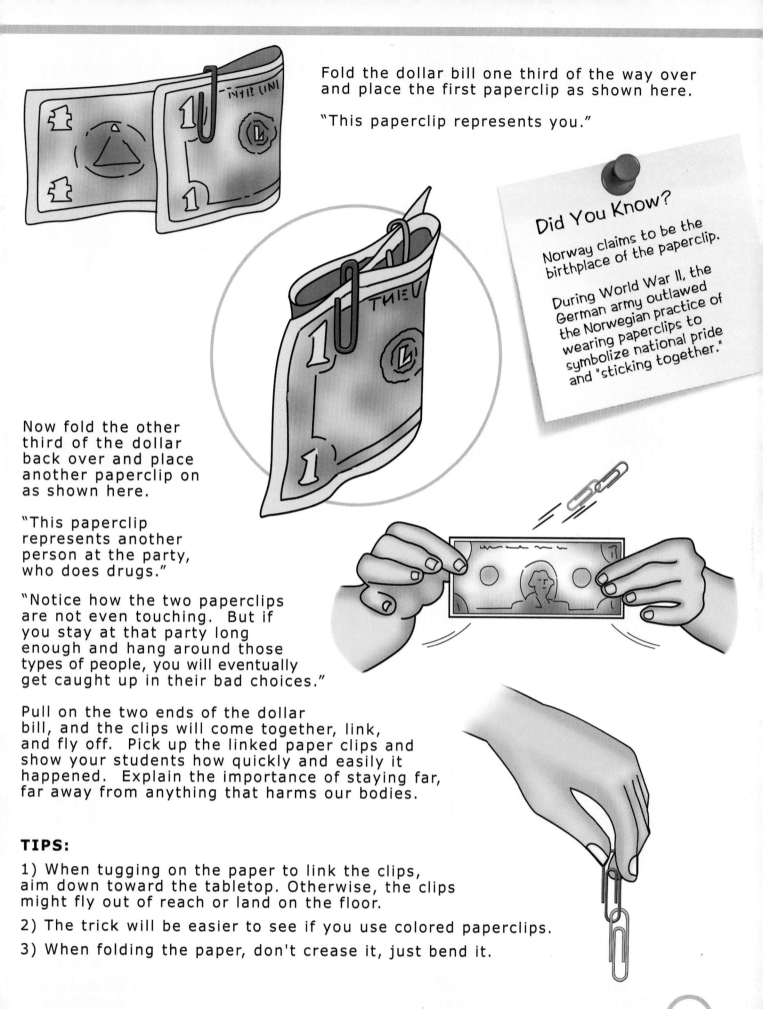

Teach by Magic believes that teaching is a noble calling and that hundreds of thousands of teachers—who could triple or quadruple their salaries if they went into the corporate world—teach because they believe wholeheartedly that what they are doing is important.

Teach by Magic shares that belief and greatly admires the teaching profession for its dedication. Our program is created to supplement the many wonderful methods that teachers everywhere have devised. Our purpose is to provide teachers with a tool, the use of magic in the classroom, which can be fun and instructive at the same time.

This book is just the tip of the iceberg, its purpose being to introduce you to Teach By Magic, the online resource. At TeachByMagic.com, you will find hundreds of tricks with many different presentations. In fact, most of the tricks in this book have multiple applications. The website allows you to watch each one so you can decide which presentation best fits your needs. We have included a small index of topics to give you a better idea of some of the applications available and how the tricks in this book can be applied to a variety of different subjects.

Aside from the obvious advantages of being able to see each trick performed and the ease of learning through videos, the site also offers the ability to browse by category and search by subject. You can sort based on level of difficulty, preparation time, and popularity. And, of course, the site offers a wide variety of downloadable printouts, a handful of which you've been introduced to in this book.

We are dedicated to continually improving the site to make it a better resource for you. We are constantly adding new videos and would welcome your suggestions. If you don't find a trick that fits your needs, please utilize the lesson request feature on the site to let us know. We'll get a member of our team right on it, and you'll be notified when your requested trick has been created.

Speaking of our team, each Teach By Magic presenter has been specifically chosen for his or her background and experience in educational magic. Many of them offer educational assemblies or are available for in-service workshops and conferences. For more information on assemblies and workshops visit TeachByMagic.com.

We sincerely appreciate your support, and we acknowledge all you do for your students. From all of us at Teach By Magic, here's one big...

THANK YOU!

Brian Daniel
- Thanks to Mrs. Morgan

Brian Daniel wishes he were from Virginia, so let's just pretend he is. He loves playing with his dog, building things out of cardboard, collecting good, clean jokes, and traveling with his incredible wife, Rebekah! For two years Brian lived in Rio De Janiero, Brazil, as a missionary, and it was there that he learned how powerful magic is as a teaching tool.

Brian has done a little of everything in magic, from performing and inventing new tricks to consulting and owning a magic manufacturing company. His many interactions with others in the field of magic allowed him to assemble some of the best minds in educational magic and establish the site www.TeachByMagic.com. Before establishing Teach By Magic, his greatest contribution to the world was inventing the boaj (www.boaj.com).

Michelangelo
- Thanks to Mrs. True

Michelangelo was given his nickname as a three year-old kid in Pocatello, ID. He loves art (of course!) and music and theater and writing. These aren't practical career choices, but they do all come together beautifully in creating magic. While he's never met a dessert he didn't like, Michelangelo considers vanilla ice cream floating in a small sea of root beer to be exquisite.

As a full-time entertainer and consultant, Michelangelo invents and builds illusions and props for theatrical productions, magicians, and other performers. Teachers have a very special place in his heart: his mother was a public school teacher for more than thirty years. He knocks the rust off his inherited skills by substitute teaching often, which also affords him the chance to try out new magic on highly-discerning student audiences. Find out more about Michelangelo at www.illusionist.net.

David Goodsell
- Thanks to Mrs. Scott

Over the past 70 years, David Goodsell pursued two careers—teacher and magican. One drove him crazy, and one kept him sane. He never figured out which was which. He has taught kids at every level, been the head of three schools, and taught elementary and secondary science methods to teachers at the university level with an emphasis in a hands-on discovery approach to science principles.

An acknowledged authority in magic, Dr. Goodsell has achieved success as a performer, an author, and a teacher of magic and, with his wife, even ran a summer Magic Camp for kids in southern California for 10 years. He is a past National President of The Society of American Magicians. For the past dozen years, he has been a regular columnist for Fun For Kidz magazine, writing articles on science activities, stunts, and puzzles.

David lives with his wife Jann, no cats, no dogs, no birds, and no fish, in Orem, UT, at the foot of the Wasatch Mountains, but he returns to the southern California beaches of his youth at least once a year.

Barry Mitchell
- Thanks to Miss Blevins

Barry Mitchell was born in Sweetwater, TN, and grew up working on a farm—or shall we say he got older while working on a farm. He loves to read books on leadership and communication, and Chitty Chitty Bang Bang is his favorite movie. He likes drinking a nice cup of hot chocolate on a cold winter morning but doesn't enjoy long walks on the beach (mostly because he saw Jaws as a young child).

Barry is a full time professional children's and family entertainer, as well as an author, storyteller, and inventor of magic tricks. His books, DVDs, and stories are used by entertainers, teachers, and ministers all around the world. Get to know Barry through his videos and discover how you too can spread educational wonder in simple, creative, and effective ways. To learn more about Mr. Barry, visit www.BarryMitchell.com.

Myke Holmes
- Thanks to Mrs. Chaney

Myke Holmes, a.k.a. "Rocus Rocus," was born in Portsmouth, Virginia. His parents were Marines, and his brothers were pesky. Fast forward 25 years, and Myke now lives in Wilmington, NC, where he loves going on adventures with his wife, Lindsey, and his dog, Sherlock. He likes eating salt and vinegar chips and watching his favorite movie, Willy Wonka and the Chocolate Factory. He also likes long walks on the beach—with SPF 85.

Myke studied acting at the world-renowned Moscow Art Theatre in Russia. He received his MFA in acting from Northern Illinois University and his BA in theatre from the University of North Carolina at Wilmington. He has been seen in various films, television shows, plays, and commercials. Currently, Myke performs with No Sleeves Magic and teaches acting at UNCW. You can find out more about him at www.MykeHolmes.com.

Mike Rosander
- Thanks to Mrs. Chaney

Michael Rosander, a.k.a. "El Mago," grew up in two completely different worlds: Miami, FL, and the mountains of North Carolina. Have you ever met a Latino with a country accent? He loves spending time with his family and friends and going on cruises, even though one time the ship left him and his wife stranded in the Cayman Islands. He also enjoys keeping track of how much money he finds in the streets and watching America's Funniest Home Videos.

Michael's interest in magic began in college while working at Tweetsie Railroad, a theme park in Blowing Rock, NC. He continued to study the art of magic as he obtained his degree in theater at the University of North Carolina at Wilmington and created a magic theater company called No Sleeves Magic. Michael now works professionally as a magician, actor, and owner of a magic camp for children. To learn more about Michael, visit www.NoSleevesMagic.com.

Mike Hamilton
- Thanks to Mr. Cutler

No stranger to educating with magic, Utah-based magician Mike Hamilton created the Magic in Learning Foundation and has gone on to perform for hundreds of thousands of students annually with his various "Magic with a Message" shows.

Mike is quick to admit that he had some learning disabilities as a young student and that's why he's always looking for opportunities to help those who might be struggling academically. He knows that everyone can learn, even if it's in a little different manner.

Mike loves outdoor activities like sky diving, fishing, camping, and archery. He's also very active in the scouting programs. His favorite thing to eat is frozen Zingers or cupcakes, but he's really known to eat most anything. He has won numerous awards for his magic, including Utah's Best of State. And if you catch his show, you just might see a live kangaroo. For more information about Mike, visit www.magicmikeutah.com.

Brian Scott
- Thanks to Mrs. Lathrop

Brian Scott grew up in Mystic, CT, and was one neat kid—that is to say, he hated to get dirty. Finger painting was not his medium of choice in art class. So it was always a surprise to find him covered head to toe in mud, wading around the coastal marsh lands of Connecticut and Rhode Island and searching for fiddler crabs and sea horses, but learning about nature had a stronger pull than staying clean. Nowadays, Brian can still be found covered head to toe in mud, but it has more to do with his two-year-old son than learning about nature, although the two are starting to mix together, albeit on a coastline 3,000 miles away from where it all started.

Brian is a professional magician, writer, and collaborative consultant, located in the San Francisco Bay Area. He has a love for all things odd and loves sharing those oddities with audiences. Brian has a simple and straight-forward approach to both teaching and learning, and you will find this throughout all of his videos. To learn more about Brian Scott, visit www.BrianScottProductions.com.

Dal Sanders
- Thanks to Mrs. Bettye James

Dal Sanders is based out of Texas, but his magic has taken him to all 50 states and several foreign countries. He loves baseball, rock & roll, and his wife and two sons. Dal has shared the stage with Bill Cosby, The Beach Boys, The Dixie Chicks, Huey Lewis and the News, Styx, Kenny Rogers, and many others. He has also appeared on television numerous times, including the station Comedy Central.

Studying and performing the art of magic full-time for over thirty years, Dal has put his entire heart and soul into his job. He is best known for his educational school shows on a number of subjects. In fact, there are many entertainers who regularly perform Dal's routines in their own educational shows. For more information on Dal, you can visit www.StageMagic.com.

Tim Manix
- Thanks to Mrs. Goen

As a youngster, Tim Mannix spent so much time at Hecklers Joke Shop in downtown Oklahoma City, they eventually hired him as a magic demonstrator. His paper route supplied money for new tricks, while the main library provided magic books that fueled his fascination with magic.

Currently, Tim presents his educational programs in schools and has taught magic to kids as part of after-school enrichment programs for the past four years.

Tim is a full-time professional entertainer, a lecturer to magicians, and a frequent performer at the Magic Castle in Hollywood, CA. He loves history, hiking, and riding his unicycle. Tim's favorite holiday is Halloween, and he carves a mean pumpkin. To learn more about Tim Mannix, visit www.FunAmazingMagic.com.

Tim Sonefelt
- Thanks to Mrs. Emory

When Tim Sonefelt was eight years old, he received his first magic set from his grandparents, and from that day forward, he could always be found in the library. At first it was because he was reading all the books he could find on the subject of magic. But now it's because he's performing at libraries all along the east coast, combining his love for entertaining and his love for books into a program that inspires children to read.

When he's not in the library, Tim enjoys NASCAR, coaching Little League, and watching Major League Baseball with his family and his good friend, Diet Cherry Pepsi.

Tim writes a brand new reading-motivation assembly for schools and libraries every year. For more information on Tim's educational assembly programs, visit www.CreativeAuthorVisits.com.

Trenton South
- Thanks to Mr. Hughes

The only non-magician in the group, and quite possibly the most interesting of us all, is Trenton South of Oklahoma. He is Teach By Magic's senior programmer and website developer. Among other things, he enjoys scuba diving, solving Rubik's Cubes, and working with wood and metal. Aside from English, he knows Armenian, Sign Language, and 15 other languages—if you count those used to talk to computers.

Trenton has a patient and understanding wife. Together they are raising their five kids, among which are two sets of twins. He earned his Eagle Scout award and still remains active in scouting. Among other notable certifications, he is a Microsoft Certified Professional Developer. To truly appreciate Trenton, you must realize that there are only 10 types of people in the world—those who understand binary and those who don't.

INDEX BY TOPIC

Life Skills

Math

Rewards/Incentives

Science

Social Studies

PRINT OUTS

The Bermuda Square

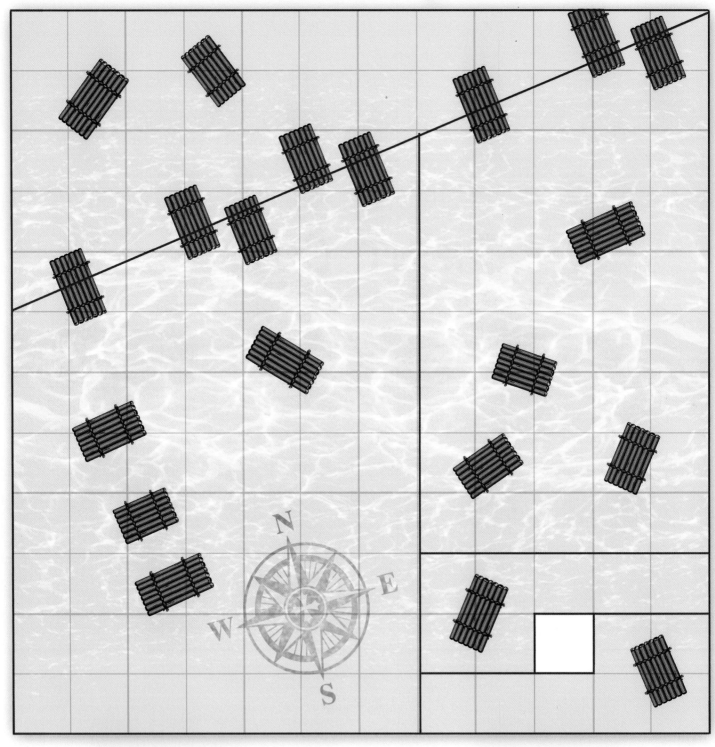

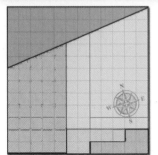
21 Rafts

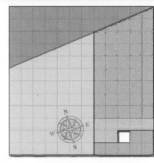
20 Rafts

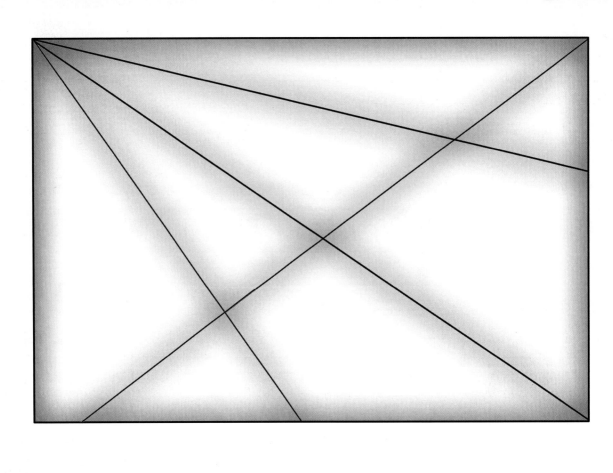

Nutrition Facts

Serving Size   Servings

Amount Per Serving

Calories   Calories from Fat

                        % Daily Value*

Total Fat	%
Saturated Fat	%
Trans Fat	
Cholesterol	%
Sodium	%
Total Carbohydrate	%
Dietary Fiber	%
Sugars	
Protein	

Vitamin A	%	• Vitamin C	%
Calcium	%	• Iron	%

* Percent Daily Values are based on a 2,000 calorie diet. Your daily values may be higher or lower depending on your calorie needs.

01	11	21	31	41	51		02	11	22	31	42	51
03	13	23	33	43	53		03	14	23	34	43	54
05	15	25	35	45	55		06	15	26	35	46	55
07	17	27	37	47	57		07	18	27	38	47	58
09	19	29	39	49	59		10	19	30	39	50	59

04	13	22	31	44	53		08	13	26	31	44	57
05	14	23	36	45	54		09	14	27	40	45	58
06	15	28	37	46	55		10	15	28	41	46	59
07	20	29	38	47	60		11	24	29	42	47	60
12	21	30	39	52	+		12	25	30	43	56	–

16	21	26	31	52	57		32	37	42	47	52	57
17	22	27	48	53	58		33	38	43	48	53	58
18	23	28	49	54	59		34	39	44	49	54	59
19	24	29	50	55	60		35	40	45	50	55	60
20	25	30	51	56	X		36	41	46	51	56	/